Is There a
Patriarch
in the House?

Is There a
Patriarch
in the House?

John L. Ward

International Standard Book Number
0-88290-246-6

Library of Congress Catalog Card Number
84-80990

Horizon Publishers Catalog and Order Number
1012

Printed and Distributed in the
United States of America
by

**Horizon
Publishers &
Distributors, Inc.**

50 South 500 West
P.O. Box 490
Bountiful, Utah 84010

THE WARD FAMILY
1982

Dedicated to my wife, Sondra, and our children:
Karl, Michael, Joel, Robert, Lesa, Amy,
Lindsay, John Allen, and Mark.
It is they who encourage me to be a patriarch in our home.

Contents

CHAPTER

I   **Is There a Patriarch in the House?** 11

II   **Different Kinds of Blessings** 17

Blessings from a Father/Patriarch 17

    Bringing Forth Children.......................... 18

    Father's Example.................................. 20

    Lost Loved Ones 21

    Father's Blessings................................. 23

    Home Dedication 25

    Family Benefits 26

    Communicating with Children 29

    Failed Parents.................................... 32

    Society's Decay 34

    Speaking Up Within the Community 35

Blessings from "The Father of Spirits" 37

    Desperate Prayers of Youth 38

    Mighty Prayer.................................... 39

    Inspired Courtship................................ 43

    Temple Marriage................................. 48

    Inspiration for Business........................... 49

    Repentance 50

Blessings from Priesthood Leadership 51

    Setting Apart and Ordinations 51

    Blessings from a Judge in Israel 52

    Blessings from the Home Teacher 56

Patriarchal Blessings 60

    Confidence Gained from Patriarchal Blessings......... 60

    Interpretation of Patriarchal Blessings 62

III   **Giving Blessings More Often**......................... 65

Questions About Blessings 65

Why Blessings Are Not Given........................... 66

Teaching About Blessings 67
Becoming Knowledgeable About Blessings 68
Being Accessible and Timely 69
Gift to Heal 73

IV   **Preparing to Give Blessings** 74
Follow Correct Procedure 74
Listen to the Spirit 76
Dress Appropriately 79
Bless When Ready 80
Wife Sustains Husband 81
Become Worthy 82
Avoid Appearance of Evil 84
Sustain Priesthood Authority 85
Speaking Up Within the Church 86
Represent Christ 87
Relationship to God and Universe 88

V   **Results to Be Expected from Blessings** 91
Immediate Results 91
Time to Heal 92
Long-Term Good 94
Learn From Suffering 96
Set New Goals 97

VI   **Conditions for an Effectual Blessing** 100
Faith of the Receiver 100
        Faith in God 100
        Faith and Works 101
Faith of the Giver 103
        Positive Faith 103
        Lack of Faith 104
        Develop Confidence 105
Priesthood Authority 106
        Power of Satan 106
        Power of the Priesthood 109
Will of God 110
        Death of Children 110
        Plan of Salvation 112

VII   **Epilogue: Open Heart Surgery** 115

Is There a Patriarch in the House?

As the sun burst over the hill on Catalina Island, I prodded stragglers in the vanishing morning fog toward priesthood meeting. The Young Adult sisters strolled in the opposite direction to the historic casino for their Relief Society meeting. Nearly one thousand Young Adults had gathered for this area conference.

A shrill voice called, "Brother Ward, Brother Ward!" Turning, I saw a frail young girl dressed in white standing in a doorway. As her Young Adult advisor I called, "You're going to be late." When she replied, "I don't feel very good, would you please give me a blessing?" I could see her feverish face. I said, "Sure, there is oil in my room—be right back." After obtaining the oil, I hurried off to the open-air priesthood meeting to get the help of another elder.

As I walked up the path to the huge outdoor amphitheater surrounded by eucalyptus trees, I was impressed by the singing of hundreds of elders. They filled the benches, and as they bowed their heads for the opening prayer I sat on an outcropping of rock. After the prayer I shook hands with another late arrival who was leaning against me as we attempted to share the uncomfortable rock. I recognized him as one of our guests, Elder Paul H. Dunn. Being that close to a General Authority, my mind focused on the previous Sunday's fireside talk where the question was asked, "If your sins had an odor, what would you smell like?" Now, sharing this rock, I squirmed as I wondered about my odor.

After an uncomfortable but inspirational priesthood meeting, I was caught up in the calm beauty of Avalon Harbor with the many white sailing boats at anchor. I walked slowly along the boardwalk, savoring the ocean sights and smells, toward the casino's auditorium for sacrament meeting. There she was, looking even more frail, standing beneath the huge arch at the casino's entrance. I had completely forgotten her! I rushed up and apologized for taking so long. I said, "Let's find a quiet place." As she walked ahead, I grabbed the nearest Young Adult and whispered, "Are you an elder? Would you please help give a blessing?" "I'd be glad to," he answered.

The only secluded spot to be found was the lounge of the women's restroom. Its avant-garde garish appearance with pink velvets, chrome, and glass was not the best setting for a priesthood blessing. Nor was the musty smell and sounds of someone being sick in the open-doored bathroom conducive to the presence of the spirit. Nevertheless, the elder and I were able to shut out the surroundings and by the power of the holy priesthood he anointed and then we both laid our hands on her head, and I blessed her to be well. The elder gave me a look of approval after the sealing and we all knew the blessing was valid.

As we shook hands with the humble, grateful girl, I noticed a tall, beautiful, older Young Adult leaning against the bathroom door. I could sense the pleading on this pale, tear-stained face. I felt compelled to ask, "Would you like a blessing?" Her eyes filled with tears. "Oh yes, would you, could you? I'd be so grateful, I'm so sick!" The Spirit of the Lord was present in the women's lounge those few moments. It became a sacred place. Leaving the lounge and entering the hallway, we were abruptly returned to the real world.

The next day on the ship heading home, the tall girl sought me out to thank me for the blessing which had healed her instantly. I took time to explain to her that it was the Lord who had healed her and we talked for some time about priesthood blessings. I was surprised and saddened at what she told me. It was her first priesthood blessing since confirmation at the age of eight. And she was from an active LDS family, too! Nor had she been set apart for the few youth and Young Adult positions she had held.

In our large family seldom a month goes by without several priesthood blessings being given. Yet this girl had never received a blessing for healing, for setting apart, for a patriarchal blessing, or blessings for other special occasions. No blessing was received when she left for the "Y", when she was depressed after her mother's death, or when "treading water" on life's decisions. Where was the father/patriarch, her home teacher, her bishop, her priesthood leader?

Well, this particular young lady had never asked for a blessing. Why? She said, "Dad doesn't like to give blessings." She was probably right. Many men, if unaccustomed to using the power of the priesthood, do hesitate. Then she added, "I just couldn't impose on someone else." She had spent this crucial part of her life without the aid of priesthood blessings with the exception of the major ones of baptism and confirmation.

Many in this church go through life without taking full advantage of the priesthood. There is no need for them to wander through life not knowing what they are foreordained to do. They need guidance in recognizing the value of priesthood blessings which are being given every day by the thousands. Most of these blessings are given by fathers acting as patriarchs within their homes. People are being healed, "lifted up," given direction, and helped in innumerable ways by bearers of the priesthood.

The priesthood blessings discussed in this book are those given by elders of The Church of Jesus Christ of Latter-day Saints. *All* fathers are patriarchs within their own homes; many unknowingly. No father can abandon that title, even when he is not functioning as one. When the question is asked, "Is there a patriarch in the house?" it refers to the priesthood bearer who may, or may not, use his authority to give blessings to his family.

To perform a blessing with "consecrated oil" and "laying on of hands," a father/patriarch must possess the "power and authority of the higher, or Melchizedek Priesthood . . . the keys of all spiritual blessings of the church" (D&C 107:18). A father is a patriarch in his house, but if he refuses, for whatever reason, to bless his family, is he a true father/patriarch? It is a tragedy if priesthood bearers fail family and God by the non-use of the powers placed in their hands. A father/patriarch may be found guilty of all the good he did not do. Jesus uttered a bitter denunciation to one who hid his talents: "Thou wicked and slothful servant" (Matt. 25:26). A faithful father will use his priesthood authority often to bless his family.

Generally speaking, we should ask for needed priesthood blessings more often. We, holding the Melchizedek Priesthood, should make ourselves available. We should occasionally suggest, through inspiration, that when a person feels ready, "Don't hesitate to ask for a blessing." Quite often hesitation is not a lack of faith, but a reluctance to impose on Dad or someone else who may appear busy or unwilling.

Once our eldest son, Karl, reluctantly knocked on our bedroom door late at night. "Come in," I said sleepily. He entered and pleadingly said, "Dad, I need to talk to you." "Sure, okay Karl," I stammered. As I fumbled for my robe my mind, now fully alert, searched for clues as to what problems my eldest might have. His application for the "Y" was due and not completed. His relationship with the family was in a downward mode. A mission was still "iffy." School was becoming more difficult. His mother (who slept soundly) could have easily doubled this list.

Feeling my way down the dark hall toward the light in the living room, I recalled how only a month ago Karl and I had had a long talk. Imagining myself to be a progressive parent, I had told my son now that he had turned eighteen he was of "legal age" and no longer had to abide by all the family rules and regulations. He had been taught correct principles and it was time for him to govern himself. Then, one week later, we had a short chat in which I told him, "As long as you live under our roof, you'll follow our rules!" At least my occasional interviews with the family had kept communication flowing. What was wrong?

Sitting across from my troubled son, I spoke first. "Karl, I love you — how can I help?" Our conversation was lengthy. He mentioned all the concerns I had imagined and more — even some that were not on Mom's list. Midway through this close, personal sharing time I felt impressed to say,

"When you feel ready some day, I'd like to give you a blessing." After we had talked and shared until there was nothing left to say, Karl asked for a blessing.

I laid my hands on his head and said, "Karl Anderson Ward, in the name of Jesus Christ, by the authority of the holy Melchizedek Priesthood, I lay my hands on your head to give you a special blessing. . . ." I paused, waiting for the right words, and with the Holy Ghost witnessing the divinity of that spoken to both of us, I continued, ". . . a patriarchal blessing to guide you now and throughout your life. . . ." Sometime later the words and tears stopped and we hugged each other. The next morning my wife learned that our son had received a patriarchal blessing. Although disappointed at not being there to record it for Karl's Book of Remembrance, she knew when she awoke that something special had happened during the night.

In the weeks that followed, Karl became an elder, decided to go on a mission, was accepted at the "Y", and received his patriarchal blessing from the stake patriarch.

Sitting in the spiritual silence at the conclusion of the stake patriarch's blessing to Karl, I reflected on how similar both blessings were. The silver-haired patriarch had revealed more about pre-earth life and after-life. My blessing revealed more about Karl's immediate future. The similarity would be astonishing to those not believing in the same source of inspiration for the words spoken. The patriarch broke the silence, telling about unseen spirits present. Then Patriarch Alvin Larsen told Karl that a father could give similar father's blessings to his children on special occasions. I caught Karl's eye and we smiled at each other.

Blessings for sickness and special father's blessings in our home have sometimes been more like patriarchal blessings. Several years ago three of our boys had colds. My wife and I took them into their bedroom. As she held a child on her lap, I anointed with oil and sealed the anointing, blessing each boy to be well. Afterwards, our four-year-old, Bobby, who was not sick, said, "Me too, Daddy." I looked at Sondra; she smiled and put him on her lap. I placed my hands on his small, adorable head and said, "Robert Craig Ward, in the name of Jesus Christ, and through the power of the Holy Melchizedek Priesthood, I give you a special blessing. . . ." I paused, feeling the spirit of the Lord, and with tears continued ". . . even a father's blessing to guide you and your parents. . . ." He received his first patriarchal blessing which was unrecorded on earth, but is remembered by us and shared with him.

After that spiritual experience, I wrote a high council talk on the need to give and receive more priesthood blessings. I felt prompted to learn more about the three gifts mentioned in my patriarchal blessings: ". . . the gift to heal, the gift to be healed, and the gift of faith." For several years, I had wanted to share my experiences to influence people to ask for priesthood blessings when needed and to help the elders be prepared, worthy, and desirous to give blessings. I had hesitated because of the sacredness of these experiences.

The world shouts over the media, "Miraculous healings!" We priesthood bearers give blessings by the laying on of hands behind our doors daily for many purposes, including healing. The Lord said, "Signs shall follow them that believe . . . they shall do many wonderful works . . . cast out devils . . . heal the sick . . . open the eyes of the blind . . . unstop the ears of the deaf" (D&C 84:65-72). Then verse 73 explains my hesitancy: "But a commandment I give unto them, that they shall not boast themselves of these things, neither speak them before the world; for these things are given unto you for your profit and for salvation" (D&C 84:73).

My eldest son, Karl, caused me to again seek the Lord in "mighty prayer" concerning the writing of this book. After conferring on him the Melchizedek Priesthood and ordaining him to the office of an elder, we spoke several times about the "how to's" of giving a priesthood blessing. Observing his awkwardness in anointing his younger sisters with oil, I was reminded again of many priesthood bearers who shy away from, or refuse to participate in, priesthood blessings. They need instruction and encouragement.

A few months after Karl's first nervous participation in a blessing, our family arrived at the home of my sister, Susan Easton, to attend BYU Education Week. During that week, nine of my family and two of my sister's children became ill. In every case, after a blessing, they were well by the following day. By participating in these ordinances before he left on his mission, Karl became knowledgeable and comfortable in giving blessings.

The answer to my prayers was to write this book as a testimony to my children and to write my journal with a theme about the power of the priesthood in prayer and blessings. My family was to know that they should, as often as needed, ask for a blessing. My sons and perhaps other priesthood bearers were to "learn how" and have the desire to give blessings.

There are thousands of homes in this church where blessings are given regularly by fathers, home teachers, and other priesthood bearers. Because we are commanded not to "boast," we may seldom learn about the magnitude of priesthood blessings. Choosing to partially reveal my experiences has been a long, prayerful searching of the soul. "Yea, I know that I am nothing; as to my strength I am weak; therefore I will not boast of myself, but I will boast of my God, for in his strength I can do all things; yea behold, many mighty miracles we have wrought in this land, for which we will praise his name forever." (Alma 26:12.)

This book attempts to document a small portion of our family's experiences with all forms of priesthood blessings; to "boast of our God," to aid our children, and possibly to aid others.

As I share many personal experiences with "the laying on of hands" as a father/patriarch and priesthood leader, the need to ask for a blessing more often is noted as well as the need to help others ask for that blessing. If fathers will develop a good relationship with their God and family, they will be asked frequently to use their priesthood powers.

This book discusses these primary relationships, the different kinds of blessings available, the need to be prepared to give them, results to be expected from priesthood blessings, and the conditions necessary for an effectual blessing. It is my prayer that the experiences of our family will help those who have ever reluctantly given or asked for a priesthood blessing.

II

Different Kinds of Blessings

When we think of a priesthood blessing, we usually think of healing the sick although other kinds of blessings with the laying on of hands may be given more often. For the purpose of discussion, the priesthood blessings presented here are in four categories: first, blessings from a father/patriarch; second, blessings direct from the "Father of our Spirits"; third, blessings from priesthood leadership; and fourth, patriarchal blessings.

Blessings from a Father/Patriarch

While serving as president of the Board of Education in Long Beach, California, a pilot high school English course was brought before the Board to be considered for regular status. After much study, the Board voted to send the course—titled "Male and Female in Literature and Media"—back to the Curriculum Committee for further review.

I was invited by a teacher to speak to her high school English class about "The Traditional Family." Prior to my visit, some students wrote letters to the local newspaper with imagined reasons for my objecting to the course. When I visited I explained to the class that I believed too much time was spent discussing social policy questions and that when controversial issues such as abortion are discussed both pros and cons should be balanced.

Then came their sharp questions: "Why not call your store Ward and Daughters?" I answered, "We don't call it Ward and Sons, we call it Ward's—a family store." "Why don't you let your wife work and you take care of the kids?" "We are happy in our current roles and it works best for us," I responded. "Why can't the father stay home and nurture the child?" they asked. Exasperated, I finally said, "Women, both physically and emotionally, do a better job and you must be unselfish enough to do what's best for the child, not what you think is best for yourself." "Well, then, just what do you do in your family?" I was tauntingly asked.

I then realized that in this old, peeling, pastel-painted classroom at Long Beach Polytechnic High School, where as a student I had sat thirty-one years before, there were now twenty-eight youth—some with no father in the home. So I told them exactly what I did in my role as "father."

"First of all," I said, "I am the patriarch of my family." Then I explained all the responsibilities of being a father/patriarch, including the giving of blessings. Upon finishing, I was given a spontaneous round of applause. One small undernourished-looking boy said, "I wish I had a family like that." I said, "Young man, it all begins with you."

Being the patriarch of a family is more than the "laying on of hands" for priesthood blessings. A patriarch presides at meals, family prayers, family council, and family home evening. He supports, educates, develops talents, and loves every member of his family. His wife is equal as they confer together in rearing the family in righteousness. Communication and encouragement flow on a daily basis. Inspiration is recognized and followed. A father provides the necessities of life and shares in family chores. A "forever family" with "a continuation of the seeds forever and ever" (D&C 132:19) is his goal. Exaltation cannot be achieved alone. By structuring a home after Christ's restored principles, and by living the commandments, a father is in a position, as patriarch, to call down the blessings of heaven upon his family.

Scripturally, "patriarch" has been synonymous with political and religious leadership. The patriarchal order is the form of government for the children of God. It is the eternal system of government. The word "patriarchal" means "family rule." Today a father is a patriarch within his own family and he "rules" in righteousness. An eternal father/patriarch presides over his posterity forever.

President Joseph F. Smith explained:

> There is no higher authority in matters relating to the family organization, and especially when that organization is presided over by one holding the higher Priesthood, than that of the father. . . . The patriarchal order is of divine origin and will continue throughout time and eternity. . . . In the home the presiding authority is always vested in the father, and in all home affairs and family matters there is no other authority paramount." (*Gospel Doctrine*, pp. 286-287.)

Bringing Forth Children

"Bless us, Lord, with children," is a fervent plea of husband and wife. How many, what kind, and when, are prayers asked to gain heavenly insight. When my wife, Sondra, began the labor pains of our seventh child, I was in a church area tennis tournament. When I got home all excited about winning my first tennis trophy my son, Bobby, told me that Sister Moore had taken Sondra to the hospital. I pushed through the maternity ward's "No Admittance" doors in Memorial Hospital in Long Beach dressed in my tennis whites, hurriedly looking for my wife. I found Sondra with my high school basketball teammate who was her obstetrician. (He has delivered most of our nine children.) Because of the severe discomfort Sondra was having, the doctor and I did not chat this time about the exploits of the old days. In fact I felt guilty about not being there to help her through labor. She had gotten a blessing from our home teacher before she left home and, when I finally arrived, she asked me for what has become a customary pre-birth blessing. Placing my hands on her warm, moist head, the blessing promised her was that she and the child would be "fine" and that this would be a "spiritual experience." Afterwards, shuddering with labor pains, she asked me to be with her in the delivery room. Previously I had been content to wait in the father's room, but because of feeling guilty about my late arrival, I said, "Sure."

By the time I was scrubbed and dressed properly, and ushered into the delivery room, the baby's head was already entering this world. I got there before the doctor did. After the excitement calmed and the baby was washed and laid next to Sondra, something beautiful and "spiritual" happened. Even the nurse said during the quiet moment, "Will you look at that!" Something passed between mother and daughter, a sign of recognition, a knowledge in the baby's eyes that "I'm where I should be, thank you for bearing me." A newly born child sees only a blur, but the eyes of Lindsay Louise (named after her two grandmothers) "lit up" with the joy of recognizing her mother. Sondra's eyes sparkled a response—a tearful, "spiritual" experience. Then Sondra told me that this had happened with each of the previous children. We had prayed for and received Lindsay and all of our children from the Lord.

We believe that God wants us to have as many children as health and our ability to care for them will allow. We have sought His will in devout prayer and we have pleaded for a special spirit to enter each tabernacle we have prepared. We are grateful for the inspired priesthood blessings that have restored Sondra's body quickly after each birth. These blessings have also assured us that God has sent to our family foreordained "choice spirits."

Raising a large family in today's society is sometimes challenging. In the early 70s when "zero population" was a media attraction, comments were made relating to our children dressed in handmade matching shirts such as "You must be good Catholics or careless Protestants." Our response was, "We're happy Mormons."

Ensuring that our children are proud of their large family is a challenge which we are meeting successfully. Each of our three girls at elementary school's Back-to-School night had pictures of their family displayed in their rooms. Our second grader happily pointed out the eleven faces painted on the wall at the far end of a bar-graph showing the relative number in each student's family. She had won!

Only once have I hestitated about being out front with my family. During my campaign for our local school board, I asked my wife, "Should we use our family picture on a hundred thousand fliers or my picture alone?" At Sondra's suggestion we prayed and, after a family council, the decision was made to use the family picture, so most of the people in the California communities of Long Beach, Lakewood, Signal Hill, and Catalina knew about "John Ward, a Mormon with lots of children." The foreordained "forever family" trying to live gospel principles can have an impact on each other and on the community, too.

Father's Example

At the time of my father's death, there was an article in the *Long Beach Press Telegram* which extolled his business, community, and church service. What stood out in the article was Karl M. Ward's "dedication to family" and that he was "first a father." As his family gathered at Long Beach Community Hospital after he suffered another heart attack at 77 years of age, we felt it was God's will that he should now rest from the turmoil of physical problems. The blessing and our devout prayers confirmed the doctor's prognosis of impending death, yet it was not a sad reunion in the hospital's waiting room. We reminisced about a wonderful father and patriarch.

I remembered him telling me how happy he and Mom were to have God send my spirit into the body they had created, and the blessing he gave me after I dumped boiling mentholatum oil on my leg, after passing out from sunburn during the Pledge of Allegiance at a scout meeting, and when he almost cut off my finger sawing a fireplace griddle. More important, perhaps, is the name of Karl Moroni Ward recorded on my certificates of blessing, baptism, and ordinations.

My father's favorite story was about how he and Mom came to California on dusty roads in a roadster with a rumble seat. In the middle of nowhere they had a flat tire which they could not fix. A man stopped, fixed their tire, and refused a token of their thanks by saying, "Pass it on." So Dad would say to us, "What I do for you, you do for your children." As he would help others, he would tell them to "Pass it on." We all felt the loss when his spirit left his body, even before the doctor told us he had just died. Before then, we had all felt his spiritual presence in our conversation. His example of being a "father first" had been "passed on."

With my Mother's help I collected all his old movies, slides, and photographs, some going back to the early 1920s. I transferred all of his pictures and my film onto video tape, heavily edited, and reduced over a hundred hours of film to nine hours of video tape. After music was dubbed in, copies were made for my Mother, brothers, and sister. This video journal of the family shows me at eight years of age with my younger brothers, Dave and Bob, standing with our Mom and Dad in front of Old Faithful in Yellowstone, near the General Sherman Tree in Sequoia, at the Pacific Ocean in Long Beach, etc. A few scenes later I am with my own young sons standing in front of the same places. The generations pass yet the earth stays basically the same.

The last scene of this satisfying project shows my six-year-old, Karl, helping his four-year-old brother, Michael, climb on a park merry-go-round. The lyrics of "Circle of Our Love" from *Saturday's Warrior* says, "Didn't We Love Him?" It was emotional for me to feel my father's love as I love my children. We do "pass it on."

The Lord has sanctioned my passing on to my children what my father passed to me. My patriarchal blessing says I will "follow in the footsteps of my father." This has literally been fulfilled. Our degree of schooling was the same: we lived in New York City and Washington, D.C.; we owned the same store; invested in apartments; were on the same high council; both were bishops; both had big families; joined the same Optimist Service Club; both ran large church dances; had the first home on the same block; were involved in the same community and politics; were both president of a business association; shared the same heart problem; had the same testimony of the restoration; etc. It is easier to be a father/patriarch if you have had a good example.

At a Father's Day conference of the Long Beach Stake, my brother, Bob, spoke about our father. The regional representative, Lloyd Rassmussen, gave an unforgettable talk about families and the geometric progression of descendants. He quoted from Genesis 18:18-19 and at one point substituted the name Ward for Abraham. It made us ill-at-ease, but the responsibility for multitudes of ancestors was implanted within us. This conference, and family video tapes, caused me to feel a greater attachment for and a bonding to my forebears and future generations; a turning of ". . . the heart of the fathers to the children, and the heart of the children to their fathers . . ." Malachi 4:6.)

A father calls forth the blessings of the Lord daily on his family in both personal and family prayer. A true father/patriarch will also magnify his priesthood power by giving blessings as in biblical times by the "laying on of hands." After baptizing five of my children and several converts, you would imagine that I could get the baptismal prayer right. Wrong! On the third try, my vivacious daughter, Amy, was finally baptized. All dressed in white she flew like an angel up onto the "stand" where she was confirmed a member of The Church of Jesus Christ of Latter-day Saints. I can still remember the power of authority and spirit I felt as I blessed beautiful, petite Amy. She, as were her older brothers and sister, was promised great things in the blessing. Her hug and warm, glowing smile will keep me worthy to do the same for the rest of my children.

Lost Loved Ones

What would it be like not to have all of your family together for eternity? The thought of not having a child with you or being unable to visit them in the celestial kingdom is heartbreaking. When my oldest son was missing at age eight, the worry was almost unbearable. He had been seen by some teenagers from church that morning, riding his bike near home. He had told them, "I'm just riding my bike around looking at all the beautiful things Heavenly Father made." Hours later, many of the ward members and neighbors were looking for him. As the sheriff's helicopter circled our neighborhood repeating over the loud speaker, "Karl go home, Karl Ward, go home!" a young searcher peered in the golf course's still, black pond and sobbed. Karl had been missing seven hours when his uncle brought him home from their unscheduled outing. Believing for only a few hours that I had lost one of my children was almost unendurable!

On a family vacation in Sequoia National Park, the older boys and I were hiking over rounded, glacier-hewn granite rocks among the giant "Red Woods." I took their pictures with my camera as they climbed higher, looking for gold in ancient potholes. I set my camera down on a gently sloping rock formation to change film. The camera began sliding down toward a cliff. On my stomach I groped for the camera. That action started my own descent. There wasn't a single crack on the rock's smooth surface to stop my slide. It was like slow motion as I struggled for a way to end my gradual journey into the unknown. I yelled at the boys for help, then shouted, "Stay back!"

I twisted around, rolled onto my back, and planted my hiking shoes flat on the slick granite. My progress slowed but I was still moving toward a drop-off to somewhere. I knew I was going over. Pressed flat on my back, clutching the camera overhead, I looked back at my children, shouted, "I love you!" and disappeared.

The edge of the rock cliff had not been a drop-off, but a steeper rounding of granite. I was able to stay on the rock as I accelerated down it. There was time to think about my fatherless family, and about me being alone without them as I fell into a large, cold-water pothole. Frightened but unhurt. I grabbed a moss-covered log and waited in the dark, narrow gorge for help, the camera still held overhead. The boys hurried down the deep ravine to gain entry to the stream, and somehow maneuvered up through the icecold water where they found me.

Later we emerged from between lofty rocks just as Sondra and the girls arrived on the scene. Sondra said, "Where have you been? You're all wet!" She tried to pull away when I gave her a big wet hug. She just didn't know how truly thankful I was to still be with my family.

A father/patriarch's goal is to lead every member of his family into exaltation where they can have "eternal increase," and become "gods and goddesses" to their posterity. The loss of a loved one, for a brief moment or for a lifetime, is a sorrowful experience, but to imagine that loss forever is to contemplate an unacceptable end. Maintaining this concept will help the father/patriarch fulfill his duty to family. Remember, "Lehi took nothing with him, save it were his family." (1 Nephi 2:4.)

Father's Blessings

The once-in-a-lifetime spiritual ordinances of baptism, confirmation, ordination, etc., for each child can be followed with the "laying on of hands" to heal the sick and for "special" blessings. A few weeks after I was diagnosed as having hepatitis after "open heart surgery," the secretary from Mark Twain Elementary School called to say our six-year-old Lindsay was ill with what to me were frightening symptoms. At home she responded to my question "Would you like a blessing?" with a weak, "Yes." I positively and without hesitation blessed her to be well that day! She was upset because I made her stay in bed when she felt "great." A week seldom passes without someone in the family asking for a blessing; particularly when they are ill.

Once while I was out of town, my wife called to tell me that our four-year-old, John Allen, had cut his hand and later the same day bumped his head hard. As he was being tucked in bed he said, "Mom, I've had a tough day." The next day, Sunday, he raised his bandaged, stitched hand when the children were asked if they had anything to say for family council. He said, "When is Daddy coming home? I need a blessing!"

Sometimes my wife asks for a special blessing when, as she puts it, "things are closing in." Having been junior Sunday School coordinator, Primary president, Relief Society counselor, Young Women's president, PTA president, etc., Sondra has occasionally needed the assurance in a blessing that God loves her and that she will succeed in her calling. Much detailed instruction, motivation, and inspiration has been given Sondra through these priesthood blessings and through her own prayers.

During an exceptionally busy time in our lives Sondra invited several of her City College classmates to our home. After they saw our children, our house and several projects a normal "Mormon home" would have, Sondra offered them strawberries as they were leaving. One overwhelmed woman said, "Don't tell me you have a garden too! You must be 'Wonder Woman.'" Doing all that a modern-day prophet and the women's Relief Society suggests a mother do is staggering to the non-member who does not understand that there has to be a husband, a patriarch, a priesthood bearer who helps, sustains, and calls down blessings on her and the home.

President N. Eldon Tanner has said:

> Every wife and mother has a perfect right and responsibility to look to her husband who holds the priesthood for guidance, for strength, and for direction. And he has the responsibility of magnifying his priesthood so he might be able to give this direction, this security, this strength that is needed in the home. And he can do this. If he will magnify his priesthood, he will be magnified by the Lord in the eyes of his family, and his influence will be felt for good. *(Conference Report,* April, 1970, p. 52.)

Once I had to leave our family's Hawaiian vacation a few days early. Sondra was so concerned as my seventeen-year-old son, Karl, drove us to the Honolulu Airport that we stopped the car and I blessed her that she would be able to "cope and care for herself and our children," and that "all would be well." She was at peace, but as it turned out, I should have blessed Karl, also.

A day later, as he made a "U" turn on the highway heading for Pounders Beach, he didn't see the camouflaged U.S. Navy fuel truck on the road below the canopy of trees. Joey and Michael both shouted, "Look out!" The truck, traveling 60 miles an hour, emerged from the dark shadows and hit the Toyota Karl was driving broadside, only inches in front of the driver's door. The massive truck overturned and skidded on its side, destroying an ancient wall.

A professor at BYU Hawaii campus had rented us his home and Toyota for our vacation. A Hawaiian, seeing the collision, and knowing the professor, took shaken Joey to tell Sondra about the accident and then drove them back toward Pounders Beach. As Sondra prayed, she remembered the blessing and knew that she would be able to "cope" and "all would be well." She saw that the front half of the Toyota was demolished. Firemen were hosing spilled fuel from the overturned gas truck. She found her two other sons in bathing suits with the paramedics, bruised but not seriously hurt. When I learned of the near tragedy, I was more upset than Sondra, who was "coping."

While I was bishop, a recent high-school graduate, Judy Centers, joined the Church. Since she was without a father's influence, she asked me to give her a special blessing as she left to serve a mission in England and later as she was soon to be married in the Los Angeles Temple. Desiring to give a similar father's blessing to my son, I waited in my sister's home in Provo, Utah, for Karl to ask for a blessing prior to his entering the Missionary Training Center. Minutes before we were to leave I suggested to Karl, "Would you like a blessing before you leave?" He said, "It can't hurt."

He received, in a father's blessing, further insight into his mission. Afterward, as we walked out the door I said, "It can't hurt." Before he disappeared into the inner sanctum of the MTC on his way to serve eighteen months in Argentina, well-tailored Karl said, "Thanks for the blessing," and gave me a big hug.

It was the same son who five years before, after a family home evening lesson on asking for blessings, said, "Dad, could I have a blessing to help me with my math?" After discussing what he should do in learning math, a blessing was given that helped until a few years later when he took trigonometry. (A blessing would have helped then, too, but he never asked.) Father's blessings may be given whenever and for whatever the Spirit may direct.

Home Dedication

Blessings may be given to help the family in many areas. Even the home itself can be blessed. At a solemn assembly held on the upper floor in the Los Angeles Temple in 1977, newly sustained Prophet and President of The Church of Jesus Christ of Latter-day Saints, Spencer W. Kimball, spoke softly with conviction to over 1500 local church leaders. I sat close enough to see him quickly shuffle through cards of "Things to Do." He had to be selective since he was not left much time on the program. Glancing at one of the cards he chose, President Kimball smiled and said, "Brethren, it is important that you dedicate your homes and ask for the Spirit of the Lord to be in them." Then he smiled again and said, "Of course, you all know what must be done before we dedicate a church building." There was subdued laughter as we realized the necessity of first paying off the mortgage.

This concept would not seem sensible to many people. My home mortgage was 6¼ percent at the time and the prevailing rate was 11 percent and climbing.

Dwelling on the possibility of having increased spirituality in our home, I shared my thoughts with my wife. As always, she wanted to do everything the prophet suggests and more. It took a while to make the final payment. When it was made, Sondra calligraphed a program with pictures of the family, home, motor home, and dog. With only our immediate family present, and everyone having speaking, singing, or praying parts we came to the time for the dedicatory prayer.

I began, "In the name of Jesus Christ and by the authority of the holy priesthood, and as patriarch of this family, I dedicate and bless this home and its inhabitants to have the Spirit of the Lord present . . ." The prayer was a long one, and referred to our home as "a refuge, a safe citadel, a place where love would abound, a place where friends would enjoy visiting, a home open to the community, but where the evil things of the world would not penetrate."

After the prayer even our teenagers had tears. If the children are asked for their most spiritual experience they will, without hesitation, say "The dedication of our home."

The presence of "something special" as Lesa described the feeling, lasted in our home for quite a while. Shortly after the dedication, I received a call from a friend I had baptized when she was a youth. She said that since her marriage she had not been active in the Church. She complained of suffering from a persistent bad cold and asked if I would give her a blessing. I suggested that she and her husband come to our home. After the blessing her husband said, "I feel something good here." Baptizing him three months later made *me* feel good.

Even now, years later after PTA meetings, Sondra will be told by those who attend, "We enjoy being in your home. There is a good feeling here." After our state senator spoke to a large education group in our house, he said, "I felt something special in your home." Thank you notes from guests will refer to "a glow."

As we go about our sometimes hectic, complicated, frustrating daily lives, our family does not always fully realize the peace in our own house. There is still occasional yelling, hurting, and bad feelings in our family. But we have become accustomed to our surroundings. Sometimes it takes a visitor to remind us that our home is, indeed, blessed.

Home is a place I rush to after work for renewal, my "quiet harbor" from the world. The dedication of our home has helped make family life easier with no serious problems with our children. We know we receive divine guidance in raising them, and that our home can be as sacred as a church chapel. In fact, we have since adopted for our home the same theme used for the Lakewood Second Ward when I was bishop: "Organize yourselves; prepare every needful thing; and establish a house, even a house of prayer, a house of fasting, a house of faith, a house of learning, a house of glory, a house of order, a house of God" (D&C 88:119).

We are cautioned about having a "restless spirit" when it comes to moving the family frequently. Moving can be harmful to a child's growth. My father described the house we purchased as "too big for your small family." After nearly twenty years in our house it has barely accommodated our family and friends but we have listened to counsel that "Whenever homes are built the thought of permanency should always be present." (J. F. Smith, *Gospel Doctrine*, p. 301.) The dedication of our home was also a definite factor in our decision not to move.

How much have we lost by paying off a low interest loan? Absolutely nothing! We have gained by heeding a prophet's voice. (The 1983 General Handbook of Instructions suggests that church members may now dedicate their home, whether or not they are free of debt.)

Family Benefits

President Peter Dalebout asked the high council of the Long Beach East Stake, "Who will volunteer to give a talk at the upcoming Saturday night session of stake conference?" The topic was the scripture "As for me and my house, we will serve the Lord" (Josh. 24:15). No one volunteered. I nominated a fellow high councilman who nominated another and so on. Since I was the first to start this "foolishness," the president chose me.

On the way home I felt unworthy to speak on this subject. After talking to Sondra, I knew many ways in which we were not fully serving the Lord. Over the next few days, however, we counted 38 things our family tries to do because of our church membership. These benefits have gradually been adopted into our family and they are bringing added happiness and security to us.

To show how our household tries to "serve the Lord" we depicted, on film, our family demonstrating these 38 benefits.

The film begins with a shot of the front of the house with the background music "Bless This House." The garage door opens to reveal our (1) year's supply of food and water. You would have to be observant to notice that the ground cover out front was strawberries, all that was left of the preceding spring's (2) garden.

The film continues in this order: (3) children in scripture study; (4) personal prayer; (5) family prayer; (6) blessing on the food; (7) fasting for a purpose; (8) healing of the sick; (9) personal family interviews (Amy promises not to call her brothers "dumb" or "stupid" any more); (10) weekly family home evenings with all its facets of gospel study, activity, talent development, etc.; (11) family council; (12) two daughters in long dresses representing our moral teachings with Lesa saying, "I wear long dresses so I can go to the temple and wear garments like Mommy"; (13) Amy saying, "Like Daddy"; (14) a commercial shows our store's sign "Closed Sunday"; (15) the children explain home rules; (16) such as "no swearing"; (17) chores and other "work experiences"; (18) Bobby showing his money jars for spending, tithing, and; (19) mission; (20) Sondra explaining why there are no ashtrays or serving of liquor even when community groups meet in our home.

The camera then shows our (21) pictorial genealogy in the hall; (22) our four-generation group sheets laid out on the pool table along with our; (23) Books of Remembrances and Grandpa explaining; (24) his life's story and journal.

Our station wagon door opens as the music "Who Are These Children Coming Down?" is heard and our newest child is introduced signifying; (25) pre-mortal life and the spirit and body together forming the soul. As the family marches into a church meeting to *Saturday's Warrior* theme song, Mike stops and says; (26) "We attend all our church meetings and; (27) serve in many church callings."

The film goes on to show or mention; (28) scouting and our belief in a divine Constitution; (29) Book of Mormon, Doctrine and Covenants, Pearl of Great Price and other church publications; (30) counseling by priesthood leaders; (31) the plan of salvation; (32) a modern-day prophet; (33) the father/patriarch; (34) patriarchal blessings; our belief in (35) good education; (36) eternal marriage; (37) the bearing of testimonies; and (38) dedication of our home.

The movie ends as our station wagon drives off into the sunset. The viewer can see our bumper sticker "Happiness Is Family Home Evening" and the children as they are singing "We Are a Happy Family."

This may sound too good to be true. Right! This film was heavily edited. The first time they sang "We Are a Happy Family" I could be heard yelling, "Sing, Michael, or I'll get you later!"

We have so much! We believe we should share these benefits of the gospel of Jesus Christ. We try never to hide them. We want to open our doors more often to let our guests experience these evolving benefits and feel "something special" inside our home.

There were other benefits from "serving the Lord" that were impossible to show in the film such as those summed up by Joseph F. Smith's statement:

> A home is not a home in the eye of the gospel, unless there dwell perfect confidence and love between the husband and the wife. Home is a place of order, love, union, rest, confidence, and absolute trust; where the breath of suspicion of infidelity cannot enter; where the woman and the man each have implicit confidence in each other's honor and virtue." (Joseph F. Smith, *Gospel Doctrine*, p. 302.)

When the Long Beach Polytechnic High School student asked me "What do you do in your family?" he really didn't know the father's role since he had never known his father. There is much in the role of being a father/patriarch that may seem mundane compared to the responsibilities mentioned, but they are also important.

I told the class, "As a father I attended Karl's choral group's performance last night and his tennis match this afternoon. Tomorrow night I am going to a scholarship assembly with Joey. Mike had his basketball team coming over so I repaired the backboard. In my monthly interviews I had noted to help Bobby with his dribbling a basketball and Lesa with throwing the baseball. Last Saturday I helped Amy ride a two-wheel bike and rescued Lindsay from our fighting dogs. We had just placed John Allen in a special pre-school to help him with his speech. Sometimes at night I tell the little ones stories, after which they know to ask 'What's the moral to the story, Daddy?' "

I believe it was for these seemingly less significant roles that the high school English class applauded although at first these roles may not appear to belong in a book which emphasizes the giving and receiving of blessings, but without such involvements will the children feel that they can ask their father for a blessing?

Close contact and coordination with the family should have first priority for a father/patriarch. Once a week on Sunday, in family council, we calendar and solve problems. On Monday night a weekly family home evening is held for instruction and recreation. Our family meets together and prays together regularly. Christ, speaking to his disciples after his resurrection said, "Pray in your families unto the Father, always in my name, that your wives and your children might be blessed. And behold ye shall meet together oft; . . ." (3 Nephi 18:20-22). We are promised in Proverbs 22:6, "Train up a child in the way he should go: and when he is old, he will not depart from it." We "meet together oft" to pray, train, and renew ourselves.

Sometimes family home evening is a disaster. Like the time several children began crying and we all piled on, pretending to cry. Everyone sings out during family gatherings and at church except me. (Once while encouraging the children to sing at church, I heard laughter from the rows behind. My two-year-old, John Allen, was sitting on my lap with his tiny fingers stuck in his ears.)

Sometimes I feel "I'm asked too much," and I get "weary of well doing" (D&C 64:33). Because I am able to regularly meet with the family, problems are eventually solved, progress is made, and love is felt. My family and I are renewed. The benefits of close family relationships are innumerable within the gospel of Jesus Christ.

Communicating with Children

Teaching children is sometimes difficult. Children often misunderstand. In trying to help the younger children understand Christmas and Santa Claus, I explained that sometimes Dad was Santa Claus. Four-year-old Amy, on Christmas Eve, said to me, "Why are you home lying around?" I explained Santa Claus again more carefully. On Christmas day I walked out front and noticed Amy sharing her toys with some of her neighborhood friends. Suddenly they dashed up to me staring in awe. "What's going on?" I said. One cute little girl holding her new doll up to me said, "Gee, thanks Mr. Ward." I said, "You're welcome." I decided to let her parents try to explain.

It is difficult to keep track of age differences and realize the passage of time. We should not speak to children below their level of understanding, but it is easy to forget. One day my wife dropped our three girls off at elementary school. As usual, she gave each one a hug and words of endearment. She then dropped off six-foot Michael at Lakewood High School for the first time in a year. As she drove up, he bolted out the door and walked toward his friends. Sondra rolled down the window and shouted, "Goodbye, Mikey, I love you." Michael slumped over as though he had been mortally wounded. Then he stood erect, waved back and with a big grin called, "Goodbye, Grandma!"

Listening to every child is important. We loaded our station wagon after our enjoyable but tiring week at family camp in the High Sierras and it wouldn't start. As the starter turned over and over with no effect, and the children became more restless, I became tyrannical. Little Bobby leaned over the back seat and said, "Ev-a-ar-a-besing, Daddy." I pushed him back before I realized what he had said—"Give the car a blessing, Daddy." So I calmed down, told Bobby I was sorry and that he had a good idea. We all bowed our heads and in that hot, humid car I offered a prayer for us and for the car. The instant I turned the key again the engine started and we enjoyed each other during the long drive home.

Anger can cause a child to be unresponsive to future suggestions of spiritual help. One vacation, as daylight faded, Michael and I went ahead with the speedboat to find a place to "land" and tie up our rented 50-foot houseboat on Lake Powell. Among the majestic, towering, mineral-painted walls of Escalante Canyon there were few places to secure the massive houseboat. Around a sharp bend in a high, narrow gorge was a sandy beach with outcroppings of rock just below the water on both sides of a landing spot. I told Michael to take me back to the slow, ponderous houseboat and then hurry back in the speedboat to save our spot.

I went up the narrow rock canyon at full speed with the houseboat intending to force this mass of metal up on the beach securely the first try. As I came around the bend, there was Michael standing on the beach holding the small speedboat in the only safe place for us to land. I threw both engines in reverse, ran to the front of the houseboat and yelled at Michael to move the speedboat. Too late! Our momentum carried us forward. I swerved to miss the speedboat Michael was trying desperately to move and the rented houseboat landed with a crunch on the rocks.

I was furious. Michael cowered under my wrath. Only as he was trying to tow us off the rocks with a line from the small speedboat did I begin to calm down. The houseboat broke free as I alternated the reversing motors while everyone else, including Grandma Ward, jumped up and down on the boat's stern.

Later that evening I apologized to my wounded son, and as we shared our impressions of this episode we began to laugh. We still laugh about it.

Sometimes when I've been harsh or neglectful I will pause for a long look at my children while they are sound asleep. Only a few years ago they were babies. Do I expect too much of them? So what if they get dirty or make a mess? Is it worth scolding them rather than to reason with them? So I kiss them and promise to do better tomorrow. (Guess what? They usually do better, too.)

President Joseph F. Smith declared:

> . . . Keep your boys close to your heart, within the clasp of your arms; . . . make them to feel that you love them, that you are their parents, that they are your children, and keep them near to you. . . . But it is when you turn them out of the house, turn them out of your affection—out into the darkness of the night into the society of the depraved or degraded; it is when they become tiresome to you, or you are tired of their innocent noise and prattle at home and you say, "Go off somewhere else,"—it is this sort of treatment of your children that drives them from you. . . . It is a crime in the sight of God and man for a father to carelessly or willfully neglect his children. (Joseph F. Smith, *Gospel Doctrine*, p. 282.)

A father/patriarch should be a leader, guide, and director. Without good communication, will your children follow you? You cannot be a leader if there are no followers.

I learned this principle as a twenty-four-year-old Army recruit. On the close-combat hill at Fort Ord, California, the Infantry Basic Training is rigorous. Groups of four soldiers dressed in army-green combat fatigues would attack the machine gun nest at the top of the 45-degree barren hill by firing blank rounds of ammunition at dummy machine guns as they ran, crawled, and dove into slit trenches, always climbing toward an imaginary enemy.

Our group of Walters, Ward, Waters and anonymous was alphabetically, as usual, the last foursome into pretended combat. By coincidence, three of us were Mormons, and since most of the company knew that, we tried harder. We attacked the hill, firing as fast as the worn World War II M1 rifles would operate. Crashing into the first trench, Waters grabbed the hot barrel of his weapon and swore. Since he had never sworn before, he looked surprised. We were laughing about it when our unloved sergeant cut short our amusement by yelling, "Go! Go!"

As we fell, out of breath, into the second dusty trench Walters lost his glasses. When he shouted back to the yelling sergeant, "I can't see where I'm going!" everyone laughed. The sergeant was swearing because we were having a hard time climbing out of the trench to "fight" our way to the last position thirty yards in front of the machine gun nest. We continued to fire. I threw a smoke bomb. The canister hit the barrel of a machine gun and bounced back down the hill toward us. We watched it roll into our trench and right to my feet where it exploded.

The smoke billowed around me. My companions began to giggle as I disappeared in the cloud. The louder the sergeant swore at us to finish our attack, the harder we laughed. Since I was the oldest I tried to continue our assault, but as I got out of the trench and reached to help Waters I saw through the smoke that he was curled up laughing. I burst into giggles and fell face first into the trench.

That did it! No one could move us out: not the old sergeant, not even the exhausted, exasperated young lieutenant who ran up the hill to demand our compliance to orders. We could not stop laughing. Even our fellow troops in the platoon got the giggles as they carried us out and down the hill. During "KP" duty the next day the four of us would laugh when we looked at each other.

Neither the sergeant nor the lieutenant could lead us because for a while we were not leadable. This is also true in our own families. We are only leaders when our wife and children allow us to be.

When fathers participate with their families and when there is open communication, enjoyment, respect, and love, then opportunities to bless their lives occur frequently. We learn by doing. We should not delegate our responsibility to someone else. "What manner of men ought ye to be?" Christ said, ". . . even as I am." (3 Nephi 27:27.) Impossible now, yes; but all that's necessary is that we be heading in His direction. Open communication will make fathers available for requests for help from the family.

Failed Parents

Many fathers abandon their families. They "flunk the final test of manhood." While I was alone in the mountains writing this book, I went into Blue Jay, California, to eat. I was seated a few feet from a father who was having dinner with his attractive young-adult daughter. Apparently she had just come to live with him and she was trying to let him know she forgave him for running off with his mistress, leaving his wife and five daughters behind. He bragged about his looks, sexual exploits, and all the things he would some day give her. She wanted his love, but he brought up her teenage mistakes, which included abortion. He ridiculed his former wife and tried to get his daughter to disavow her mother. Then he began to pour out his problems to his daughter instead of giving her the help she asked for. He appeared to want his daughter's understanding, honor, and love, yet he was "turning her off." In essence, he was saying, ". . . if then I be a father, where is mine honour?" (Malachi 1:6.) He was losing from his daughter what little love and respect remained. At this point I couldn't eat any more and I left.

We have our parents to thank or blame for our heredity and environment. To a large measure we are products of their influence.

In my missionary journal the following is recorded:

> At the end of three months we ran out of good tracting area in Barnsley in a Yorkshire county of Northern England and moved out to Athersley Estate. Oh brother, what an ordeal! The coal miners ('work down pit') were friendly, but many of the homes were so filthy that the smell we received while standing on the doorstep was unbearable. Our hearts would become heavy when we would see a beautiful, fresh youth enter one of these homes and be greeted by an unkempt mother or father. In time the child would also lose the spark of spirit which should be evident in the eyes. Environment means so much. Athersley Estate made us thankful for our homes!

While I was on the school board I received a weekly report from the School Attendance Review Board of children who were missing most of their classes. The description of these children's living conditions and the uncaring attitude of parents toward them was appalling. Children were kept home to take care of their mother's alcoholism or drug needs. Fathers had disappeared, and the welfare money was squandered in the pursuit of bodily pleasure. It made no difference whether the children were in school or not. A few of the hundreds of cases were grateful for help because they were destitute or unfamiliar with the language and culture. Most, however, had willingly abandoned their children, either figuratively or actually.

Every time I read the details of this report I thought of the scripture, "But whoso shall offend one of these little ones which believe in me, it were better for him that a millstone were hanged about his neck, and that he were drowned in the depth of the sea" (Matthew 18:6).

Most of the families on the School Attendance Report were poor, but even the rich abandon their children. After high school I became the camp director of SA-HA-LE Lodge in Big Bear, California. My brother, Dave, and I had a "blast" running this private camp of mostly rich kids. The parents had left them there for a few weeks, some for the entire summer. It was obvious to me, as some cried and told me of their home life, that their parents were "getting rid of us" as one youth said.

Many children escape their environment by running away. One evening I was called out of a church meeting to answer the phone. Sondra said a ten-year-old girl who had run away from home knocked on our door. When she answered it this girl, who was afraid of the dark, said "Do you want a daughter?" Sondra asked me, "Can we keep her?" We had four boys then and were praying for a daughter. I said, "Honey, find out her name, address and phone number. Keep her there. I'll be home in an hour."

At home Sondra told me the girl's pitiful story. Her older brother had run away again the day before. Her parents were alcoholics. She had probably been abused. We called the sheriff's office at 10 p.m. No missing child had been reported but they would send a car for her. We gave them the information we had about her home and abuse. Sondra talked to me about possible adoption. She already loved this lonely little girl.

The girl was allowed to stay with us until the next morning when the sheriff called to say the parents were on their way to pick her up at the sheriff's station. She clung to protective Sondra when she saw her dissipated-looking parents waiting in front. As the parents approached Sondra she hurriedly walked past them and, reluctantly, turned the sad girl over to the sheriff. Laws protect parent and child. Pity the child of an abusive parent.

Every child in God's plan should have a loving, caring mother and father; yes, even a patriarch in the home. I was so concerned about this subject, I used it at a vespers talk at Lakewood High School. I told the graduating class of '82, "If you choose to have children, then care for them. Do not pursue personal pleasure or intense careers to the detriment of your children." With more mothers working, what is happening to the children? The ravages of child neglect are all about us.

A major purpose of man's life on earth is to learn to be a good father. Sometimes we may feel we are in the "refiner's fire." At the end of life perhaps we have gained some of the qualities of fatherhood that we needed before we became a father. We must try to be better fathers today than we were yesterday, and better fathers tomorrow than we are today.

At the very least we should start by providing adequately for our families. A man must spend time in the business of making a living for himself and his family. A father should strive for increased financial independence. The apostle Paul said, "But if any provide not for his own, and specially for those of his own house, he hath denied the faith, and is worse than an infidel" (1 Tim. 5:8). We provide food, clothing and shelter. Add to this, time—time for our family and we are "on our way" to becoming a true father/patriarch. As Mark Twain said, "If at first we don't succeed—fail, fail, fail." We cannot abandon our family. In today's society the father is needed more than ever in his patriarchal role.

As a busy new parent it was challenging for me to ponder, "Just what is the proper role of a father?" It took years for me to absorb the words of prophets and have the following priorities imbedded in my conscience. A father should:

First, progress spiritually, emotionally, and physically.

Second, love wife and children and meet their individual needs.

Third, render diligent service in all church callings.

Fourth, earn a decent, honest living.

Fifth, contribute to the community in a positive manner.

On a daily or weekly basis it is easy to reverse these priorities. A father should frequently assess his performance.

Society's Decay

I once attended a gospel doctrine class in Provo, Utah, where the question was asked, "Is society worse now than in our grandparent's day?" Some said "Yes," others said "No." Not one to remain silent, I said, "A sign of Christ's coming would be '. . . as the days of Noah were . . .' (Matt. 24:37), which tells me it's worse now and deteriorating." I told the class, "My father never had to call the vice squad to round up the prostitutes and dope pushers in front of our store. Mom didn't need to lead a community drive to close a drug 'head shop' two blocks from the children's high school. In one month, five murders were committed within four blocks of our store; my parents never had their store or home burglarized once, let alone several times. Even our missionaries are not allowed to tract some nearby urban areas. There were no television assaults on our morals or readily available pornographic publications. Did any of our ancestors fight to remove an X-rated theater from their neighborhood?"

Once, when I was caught up in fighting many different causes, I was asked to give the invocation at my weekly Optimist Service Club. My prayer to help youth overcome these problems was long, so I was good naturedly booed. At Optimist Club, our respected community rabbi showed me a T-shirt lettered with "Eat, drink and be merry for tomorrow you may be in

Utah." Perhaps some families in Utah are more sheltered from society's plunge into decay, but "even the very elect shall not escape."

President Harold B. Lee has given this counsel:

> I was in California, where we had some anxious parents . . . (who) wondered if they should move . . . to the Salt Lake Valley to get away from the influences that seem to be crowding in upon them. . . . And I said, "Now the all-important thing for you folks is not where you live, because you cannot escape the power of evil; but the all-important thing is how you live. If you folks want to be protected during this time of stress, you have given you in the gospel of Jesus Christ the fundamental principles by which you can be saved. If you will have your family home evenings and teach your children in the home, the promise has been made that there won't be one in a hundred that will ever go astray . . ." (Harold B. Lee, Address at BYU Sixth Stake Conference, Apr. 27, 1969).

If there was ever a time for patriarchal order, for strong inspired mothers and fathers who are close to and love their children, it is now. Parents need to fight the decay in their communities. They must make their homes a refuge, an island of safety. When the Nephites were contending with a large force of evil invaders, the Lord said for them to ". . . defend themselves, and their families, and their lands, their country, and their rights, and their religion" (Alma 43:47). Do not accept the decay about you. Fight back. Be involved. Set aside ". . . time for family members, as citizens, to take part in improving their community and strengthening the process by which people of integrity are elected to public office." (From February 1, 1980, "Sunday Meeting Consolidation Letter" signed by the First Presidency.)

Anciently, King Mosiah taught his people that "the burden [of righteous government] should come upon all the people, that every man might bear his part" (Mosiah 29:34).

As father/patriarch lay hands on the heads of your family to bless them in confronting the host of temptations that lie in wait. As the family patriarch, be inspired to recognize any subtle decay within your home. By accepting the mantle of authority placed upon you as father/patriarch, the Lord will bless you to succeed in saving yourself, your family, and possibly some within your community.

Speaking Up Within the Community

The ability to lead, learned while serving our families and church, enables fathers and mothers to be natural leaders within their communities. Balancing family, church, work, and community service must be carefully planned. Reconsidering a previous announcement to campaign for the California state senate, I wrote in my journal during a period of tough decision-making on June 18, 1983, "Writing my book has made me, more than ever, want to be a father first. President Brigham Young has said, "To be a successful father . . . is greater than to be a successful general or a successful statesman!" While leaving the auditorium of Mark Twain Elementary School after another meeting in our six-year struggle with X-rated films at the Lakewood Theater, I told a friend my decision: "Someone else will have to fight the battle of pornography, drugs, crime, education, et cetera, in the legislature. My family comes first!"

Even as I wrote that journal entry it did not sound right, nor did it when I discussed it with Sondra. I want to do what is right for my family, but can I abandon society? What about society's influence on my family?

On June 20, 1982, I wrote, "By invitation from the Secretary of Education, Dr. Bell, I attended an educational gathering at Pioneer High School in Whittier, California. There were hundreds of cameramen with bright lights focused on the middle of the basketball floor. Distinguished-looking educators and politicians were crowded in the bleachers waiting for the arrival of the President of the United States.

"Members of the President's Commission on Education entered first. Dr. David Gardner, Chairman of the Commission and newly appointed president of the nine California state universities spoke first. We had attended BYU together. He introduced the Secretary of Education, Dr. Bell, a member of the President's cabinet, a Mormon. Dr. Bell introduced the California State Senate Minority Leader, William Campbell, another Mormon.

"We could hear the helicopter landing; more reporters rushed in; then everyone gave a deafening cheer as President Reagan entered enthusiastically. It was some time before the happy, boisterous crowd allowed the President to speak. He praised the work of the three 'Mormons' just introduced (not by this title). President Reagan gave an excellent talk in which he said 'No success in the schools can compensate for failure in the home.' (One of the President's speech writers is also a Mormon.)"

Prophecy tells us that the priesthood will be recognized in the affairs of mankind. Priesthood bearers are to defend the inspired Constitution in the last days. Just as fathers progress slowly in their priesthood responsibilities in the family, so also is the priesthood gradually being recognized in increasing numbers and effectiveness in federal, state and local government.

After the morning at Pioneer High School, my desire to reform and fund public education is greater than ever. I want to change society for the better! In rereading my journal quote of "Someone else will have to fight the battles" it rings hollow. Sure, it's greater to be a successful father than a successful statesman, but it was Brigham Young, a very successful statesman and father, who said it. The three "Mormon" men at the Pioneer High School's meeting are successes at both. If we use the excuse of staying home with the family because it comes first in our father/patriarch role, then who is to run our government, jobs, and church? Yes, when we are needed at home we should be there, but we are also needed at work, at church, and where laws are made, especially those laws that will have an impact on our family, church, and jobs.

Laws are made every day in our cities, states, federal government, and courts. Can a father/patriarch afford not to become involved? How can he be passive about laws that would destroy the family unit, allow immorality, weaken the constitution, take away freedoms (including worship), waste taxes, etc.

Joseph Smith gave counsel regarding the value of using influence for good:

> It is our duty to concentrate all our influence to make popular that which is sound and good and unpopular that which is unsound. "'Tis right, politically, for a man who has influence to use it, as well as for a man who has no influence to use his." (*History of the Church*, 5:286.)

Our local assemblyman was quoted in the newspaper as saying, "A family man should not be elected to the legislature. The time away from home, the travel, the trials will destroy even the best of families." If he's right, are we to be represented only by single men and women? Who will represent the children? Already this nation has seen the horrendous effects of children and families being under-represented where laws are made.

Most fathers would never consider becoming politicians themselves, but all fathers ought to vote and give their input to local politicians. Not to do so allows well-organized, vocal opponents of many things we hold dear to ultimately get their way.

A father can be a leader in the community, church, or workplace and still be a successful father/patriarch if being a "father first" is his number-one priority, and he shows that it is. "No other success can compensate for failure in the home." (President David O. McKay in Conference Report, Apr. 1964, p. 5.)

Blessings from "The Father of Spirits"

Our Eternal Father, Elohim, is the father of our spirits. "Furthermore we have had fathers of our flesh which corrected us, and we gave them reverence: shall we not much rather be in subjection unto the Father of spirits, and live?" (Hebrews 12:9.) Of all the mighty descriptions of God within the scriptures, God himself chose to be called "Father." There is no higher honor than to be a father. A favorite hymn of our family is "I Am a Child of God." God the Father wishes to bestow blessings on His children. Should we not seek His direct blessing first before we "call for the elders"?

"Be thou humble, and the Lord thy God shall lead thee by the hand, and give thee answer to thy prayers" (D&C 112:10). We should pause before asking for a blessing by the "laying on of hands." Have we first sought the Lord in humble prayer realizing that "The effectual fervent prayer of a righteous man availeth much" (James 5:16)?

A family friend to whom I had given a blessing before asked for another in regards to a business decision she needed to make. I asked, "Have you inquired of the Lord?" (1 Nephi 15:8). We talked at length and I suggested she study it out further in her own mind, fast, and pray for inspiration. I refused the blessing tactfully because my inspiration indicated that she needed to do as Alma, who ". . . labored much in the spirit, wrestling with God in mighty prayer, that he would pour out his Spirit" (Alma 8:10).

An elderly lady who lived behind our store asked for repeated blessings until she was taught how to pray and get answers on her own. We, who give blessings, must be cautious not to do for family or friends that which they can do for themselves through humble, fervent, mighty prayer, assuming they know how to commune with God the Father.

In this section we examine how we learn to pray in our youth and how we develop faith that God will answer our prayers. By the time we select our eternal spouse, we should be able to recognize God's answer to prayers and make correct decisions. Since choosing the right companion affects so completely a father's ability to function as a patriarch, this section focuses on inspired courtship and marriage. Heavenly help in the work place and repentance is also examined. The "Father of our spirit" blesses all areas of our lives with direct answers to our humble, personal, righteous supplications.

Desperate Prayers of Youth

I remember my first fervent prayer when I was seventeen years of age. I had driven the SA-HA-LE Lodge open-bed truck on a fire-road at a 7800-foot elevation to let the thirty kids view a fire on the other side of Big Bear Mountain, California. Proudly plump "Big Ma" Morris, the camp owner, who was sitting beside me, said, "Turn around and head back so we won't be late for dinner." I began driving down the seldom-used rocky fire-road looking for a place with room enough to turn. As the grade got steeper, the road narrowed and became deeply rutted. The fortunately thin camp nurse, who was also in the cramped cab, began to whimper as she looked into the deep canyon on her side. Big Ma said, "For heaven sakes, John, stop!"

As they discussed the coming darkness, the impossibility of backing out, the distance someone would need to go for help, I prayed fervently. Many hours later, after moving rocks and filling ruts we slowly inched our way down the deserted fire trail to the deathly dark desert. When we finally reached Victorville, Big Ma called the rangers to tell them they could end their frantic search while I found a secluded place among some huge rocks to thank God. ("Most fun of the whole summer," reported the kids to their apprehensive parents.)

Even though I had witnessed and participated in many prayers and blessings as a youth in my family I was not sure about direct answer to prayer. Besides, God had not responded to my frequent prayers about freckles, acne, and being skinny.

It was during my first year away from home that I truly learned to communicate with and depend on God. It was lonely in the crowded, noisy "D" dorm barracks at BYU. College was a challenge for a shy freshman trying desperately to "come out of his shell." I wrote my parents on the night before finals:

May 27, 1953

Dear Family:
As I approach the end of this school year, I can't help but get on my knees each night and thank the Lord for all the blessings he has bestowed on me and for my wonderful parents. When things begin to go wrong and I'm ready to give up, I humble myself before God and do what you would have me do. Never before have I depended on God so much. I know that without his guidance and my faith, I would not be ending this year successfully. I've caught the "spirit of the Y." It's something that can't be explained; but it makes you humble, proud to be a Mormon, and a "Y" student. I've always taken this gospel of ours for granted — never realizing its importance. But now I can truthfully say *I know* that this is the only true church and that I will teach the gospel to others and try to live up to all its standards. What I'm trying to get across is that I'm beginning to know God.

Mighty Prayer

When I was a sophomore at BYU, I engaged in my first "mighty prayer." Brother Reid Bankhead's large "Introduction to the Book of Mormon" class topic one fall day was Moroni 10:4-5: ". . . by the power of the Holy Ghost ye may know the truth of all things." I certainly wanted to know if the things I was being taught were true. I was planning on a mission; my girlfriend was planning on marriage. I needed help!

Driving my metallic-green "lowered" 1942 Chevrolet up Springville Canyon, I parked and climbed to a ledge that overlooked Utah Lake and the multiple mountains of the Rockies to the southeast. I knelt — for the first time outdoors — and spoke vocally in prayer. After a few hours I was asking ". . . with a sincere heart, with real intent, having faith in Christ . . ." (Moro. 10:4).

A purplish-red sunset brought darkness — a darkness gradually lit by millions of blinking stars. Mistaking emotion for spirituality because my surroundings were heavenly, I expected the heavens to open and receive my supplications. Angels were sure to appear momentarily. Nothing happened; it was getting cold; doubts entered my mind; the tears flowed and I began to sob and to beseech the Lord about my testimony and important decisions.

I climbed a little higher, looking for a place to kneel where it wasn't so damp. Exhausted, I sat on a flat rock and watched the night. Then I realized there was writing on the hard rock. It was too dark to read. My imagination went wild. Was this a heavenly message? I was now seeking a "sign." Had I

found it? Tracing the letters with my trembling finger, I found that it spelled
SPORTS POINT.

I was not disappointed; in fact, a scripture entered my mind about it
being "An evil and adulterous generation [that] seeketh after a sign" (Matt.
12:39). Laughing out loud at my foolish imaginations and looking down on
where I had knelt hours before, I began to understand. My prayers were
heard! As I exercised my faith, "all would go well."

No priesthood bearer could have laid hands on my head and given me
the knowledge I gained from that experience. Sometimes we must experience our own partial Gethsemane.

I returned to *Sport's Point* fifteen years later to thank the Lord for so
completely answering this first attempt of mine at "mighty prayer." It had
taken me that long to fully recognize His direction. Recognizing the Lord's
guidance in my life began with the following experience:

Sondra and I, with our two small boys, had recently moved into the
Long Beach California East Stake so I recognized the stake president,
Raymond Linford, when he came into our store's busy "12-hour sale," the
first of April, 1967. He said, "Brother Ward, may I speak with you? I'll not
take long." We went into my office and he flat-out asked me if I was worthy
to be the bishop of the Lakewood Second Ward. I was astonished, and hesitated since my wife and I were barely speaking to each other.

We had celebrated our Fifth Anniversary by shopping for a chandelier.
When we shop for furniture, it is at the Los Angeles Furniture Mart, a block-
square 12-story building with innumerable selections. We were impatient
with each other by the time we got home. The next day Sondra called me at
work to get my opinion on bringing home a stray, pregnant cat. "Absolutely
not!" I stated tactlessly, while in the pressure-cooker of work. When I arrived
home I opened the garage door and heard a "meow." I did not speak to my
wife that evening, or the next day. She responded by not speaking to me. I
could feel Satan's influence entwining itself in our home.

On Wednesday, four days later, Sondra went to Relief Society and that
night she touched me with her toe. A spark of spirit began to be felt for the
first time in four days. Now here it was Thursday evening and I was being
asked to be bishop and help others with their problems and I had hardly
been speaking to the future "mother of the ward" for several days.

I did not share these reasons for my hesitation with the president since
customers were waiting. I told him I would like time to repent, prepare, and
pray about it. He said, "Fine, I'll be at general conference till Monday." On
the spur of the moment I said, "My wife and I are going to conference, too."

Sondra and I knelt in prayer together that night, dumbfounded at how
we had let Satan enter our lives. He knew the calling was coming—I did not,
but could have.

On the way to general conference, Sondra told me that while she was praying she knew I would be called to be bishop the night before I was asked. We apologized, felt the wonderous effect of sincere repentance, and hugged each other.

After we arrived in Salt Lake City, I met with Elder James A. Cullimore in the old church office building. We talked about my apprehensions, sins, and testimony. Then we talked about the retail business which was his former occupation. As I descended the marble stairs, I floated on air knowing I was worthy and able to be a bishop.

That afternoon I notified the stake president and left Sondra in the Salt Lake City motel since she understood the significance of my wanting to return to *Sport's Point.* It was lightly snowing as I climbed on the ledge overlooking much of Utah County. Standing on the nearly buried engraved rock, I imagined myself as a confused college student kneeling on the spot a short distance below. Tears came as I fully realized that the Lord had heard and answered every righteous request I made during that long night. Now, fifteen years later, I laid out the towels from the motel to keep me dry from the snow-covered ground, expecting to once again pray into the night for help as bishop, husband, father, businessman, etc.

This time I began by thanking the Lord for hearing my former prayers and for guiding me through college, mission, graduate school, army, church positions, business, marriage, children, and investments. I could clearly recognize his hand in everything I had accomplished. It surprised me when I said, ". . . and continue to help me do what's right—in the name of Jesus Christ, Amen." I had not pleaded for God's help as I had done so many years ago. I knew I had it! My relatively short prayer was one of genuine thanks!

As I stood this time on *Sport's Point,* it stopped snowing, the dark clouds opened, and piercing rays of bright white light fell on me. Fifteen years ago I might have accepted this as a sign. Now I recognized the spectacular event for what it was—simply the breaking up of the spring storm, for rays of light were beginning to strike all over the valley.

I pictured in my mind a humble college student kneeling below me pouring out his heart. I wanted to say to him, "Your prayers are heard. Exercise your faith and all will go well." I said another short prayer of thanks and returned unexpectedly soon to the motel. "You okay, honey?" Sondra said. "Couldn't be better," I replied.

There was another time in my life I climbed a mountain to pray. During the Korean War there were quotas on missionaries. It was frustrating waiting two more years for a call. Finally, after a tough missionary interview with Apostle George Q. Morris, my call came April 19, 1956. The timing of the call allowed me to graduate from BYU and immediately enter the mission home in Salt Lake City. While I was in the crowded mission home, I hungered for the deep spiritual testimony evidenced by those who spoke to us.

There were a few days between the arrival of the train to New York City and leaving the mission home, so I headed for the mountains behind "Y" mountain to have a spiritual experience.

I hitch-hiked in the hot, humid July sun to Provo. Borrowing a former roommate's sleeping bag and hiking clothes, I headed up the gully to the right of the "Y." Having learned that fasting excluded water, going far without resting was more difficult. As night settled and there was still a long way to go to reach the still green meadows on top, I braced myself against a pine tree and fell asleep. Awake and gagging from lack of water I prayed emotionally, dedicating myself again to Christ's service, and sought help in getting down the steep mountain. My descent was slowed by crashing through dead bushes. Coming to the first house, I turned on the outdoor faucet and drank and drank and eventually reached my friend's home.

I tell this story to show that my motives were correct, even if the preparation for a spiritual experience was poor. There was "real intent and faith in Christ." Was I seeking a sign? Possibly I was, but also I sought the inspiration from the Lord to help others, or so I thought. The results of searching for this spiritual experience on "Y" mountain took place two weeks later at the mission home in London.

The venerable Queen Mary, now a museum/hotel in my hometown, crossed the Atlantic Ocean with a dozen anxious missionaries. We arrived at the Old Tudor Mission Home on Nightingale Lane, in London, July 12, 1956. After dinner of Yorkshire pudding, Brussels sprouts, and mutton, we went with trepidation to Speaker's Corner at Marble Arch, Hyde Park. All about us were church representatives, political groups, and "crazies" proclaiming their cause from homemade stands. It seemed like only a few tourists paused in the suffocating fog to listen to the tirades. In the middle of the confusion, an elder from the mission office unfolded, to the horror of some of us, a "soap box" with our church's name on it. Hesitantly we new missionaries stepped up on it, one at a time, to courageously proclaim the Restoration.

A fairly large group began to gather about us. One heckler kept shouting, "Eighteen hundred years too late!" The shouting by some and the cruel, double-edged questions took their toll. By the time I bore my testimony, I was scared and mad. I timidly stepped up to the makeshift podium and then with sudden resolution shouted, "My companions and I . . . ." hopefully in righteous anger continued ". . . haven't come six thousand miles at our own expense, leaving our families and friends, to be ridiculed by hecklers. May I tell you about the greatest thing in our life and perhaps yours?" They were quiet as I bore the first of my hundreds of testimonies in England. Little did I know that in the coming weeks many of those hecklers would become my "good old blokes."

I remember vividly stepping down off the "soap box" and coming face-to-face with an ugly, wild-eyed man who cursed me in a hideous-sounding language, then drove a long pin through both his cheeks. As we returned to the mission home I felt exhilarated even as my companions discussed this grotesque Luciferian who worshiped Satan.

That night there was a shortage of beds at the mission home, so I volunteered to sleep in the huge antique tub to be alone. Making my bed of down-feather quilts in this ornate bathroom, I began to feel the effects of the day's events. I knelt and expressed my gratitude for finally being on a mission and asked for help from heaven and for confirmation that I was doing the Lord's labor. As I lay in the comfortable tub alone in the bathroom, I began to cry. A soft wind blew in the windowless room. My heart and mind were filled with an overwhelming love of the Savior. His presence was felt. I lay there not wanting to move, wishing that this glorious feeling might linger. The divinity of Christ and the restoration of His gospel by the Prophet Joseph Smith were branded into my soul. The warmth of the wind subsided and I lay there overjoyed. I obtained the knowledge for which I had sought in my supposedly fruitless, aborted climb up "Y" mountain.

Even now as I write this I "tingle all over" and wipe my eyes because the memory, the feeling, and the testimony have not faded. Eventually I got out of the tub, thanked the Lord profusely, and promised him I would never seek a "sign" again: nor have I.

No vision, miracle, or supernatural event could have penetrated my soul and memory as did the witness of the power of the Holy Ghost. This is a gift given to each one who is confirmed a member of the Church. As we use this gift to benefit others our ability to give inspired blessings increases.

Inspired Courtship

As the high council advisor to the young adults in the Long Beach California East Stake I became aware that a few elders were using the priest-hood blessing, or their "right to receive revelation," improperly in seeking a mate: they would pronounce their "revelation" of marriage to an unsuspecting young lady. In many cases, emotions were mistaken for inspiration. Both parties of a "marriage made in heaven" should receive their own personal inspiration.

Choosing your eternal partner is worthy of "mighty prayer," sought-for counsel, and perhaps a priesthood blessing by father, home teacher, or bishop. The decision must be sustained by God. The "seed will grow" if it is good. "Your bosom shall burn within you" (D&C 9:8-9) at the knowledge that you have found "the one."

A relative of mine was once approached in the celestial room of a temple by an acquaintance who shocked her by saying, "It's been revealed to me—you are to be my wife." She said, catching her breath, "Why don't you begin first by asking me out?" She later refused his request for a date.

Watching young adults seek for an eternal mate, I wondered why so many came to events so poorly groomed since it is appearance, usually, that initially attracts the opposite sex. Then I would wonder why some could not see beyond the physical appearance to the more important qualities needed for a lasting, happy marriage.

In my role as family/patriarch, I explored with Karl his desire to date when he became sixteen. We talked about dating several girls (not going steady) while in high school and about being creative in dating. He followed counsel. His abilities, personality, and talents improved dramatically.

The inspired counsel I give to his brothers and sisters may be different, but we will sit down and reason together. Let's avoid some of the pitfalls of youth. A grievous tragedy for some youth is pre-marital sex leading to early marriage, abortion, or fatherless children and all the agony that comes from being immoral.

Father/patriarchs should talk to their sons and daughters; explain, with mother's help, the "birds and the bees." This is always an interesting discussion during family home evening. Help your children seek after ". . . anything virtuous, lovely, or of good report or praiseworthy . . ." (Articles of Faith, 13). If parents are timely and lovingly frank in their discussions with their children, then the children will be willing to communicate openly with father and mother.

The lack of faith in my wife's and my teaching of our children became evident two months before Karl's eighteenth birthday. One evening a man at our front door told my wife, "My daughter and your son have a problem. May I speak to your husband?" Sondra told me the father of Karl's girlfriend was at the door and seemed very upset about a problem they had. I took the concerned parent into our bedroom where he said, "We have a problem. Your son just picked up my daughter and accidentally left the car in gear and drove through our garage door." I was so relieved!

As our children become young adults can they still confide in us? Certainly we will back off as they "govern themselves." Do we also indicate to them that we are no longer their patriarch who counseled and blessed them? We will always be an effective father/patriarch, no matter the age of our children as long as they let us. As they make major decisions about schooling, courtship, and marriage they may need our blessings more than ever. We should take time to talk with them and understand their changing desires.

My search for a wife may give insight into finding a choice companion by inspiration. While in the cold, smoke-laden coal mining town of Barnsley, England, I received a "Dear John" letter from the girl who helped prepare me for a mission. It said, "I have found him. . . ." With only a two-week premonition, my girlfriend was engaged to be married. While I was carefully writing her my response, clouds outside blackened, lightning struck, and thunder echoed my inner turmoil. After her marriage, maintaining Yorkshire tradition, the missionaries of the Sheffield district gave me a "lost-a-girl doll" with my girlfriend's name inscribed on it. Since it was Guy Fox Season—a celebration with fireworks—I attached "bangers" and a three-stage rocket to the doll. As it soared upward across the fog-covered moors, it exploded! I wasn't bitter, just terribly hurt!

Graduate school began, after my mission, at New York University. The nine-month rigors of a master's degree program and work left me little time to date. Then it was home to join the U.S. Army 306th Psychological Warfare Battalion. As I left for basic training at Fort Ord, a new friend showed me his address book of pleasures. That first night in the barracks, as I experienced all the filthy talk and actions, I thought, "Will I morally survive the next six months of active duty?" "Not without help," I said out loud. I knew the Spirit would withdraw if I succumbed to temptation and, without inspiration, the chances of finding "the one" would be nil. So, flat on my back, I began one of those "heart-felt" prayers (this time silent) that I had become accustomed to on my mission.

The next day, while I was standing in a mess line, a formation of new recruits came marching by. There in the middle was a soldier with a big smile that made his eyes squint. It's best not to have favorite missionary companions; however, few missionaries have tried harder and learned more from each other than Elder Brent Brockbank and I did. It had been two years since we had seen or heard about each other.

I pushed into the formation with the sergeant yelling at us as we hugged. Not only were Brent and I at Fort Ord together, we ended up in the same company and—would you believe—the same platoon? The prayer of desperation that first night in the Army barracks made my six months of active duty productive and even uplifting.

After I was discharged from active duty, I drove home from Washington, D.C., during one of the worst snow storms on record. There was time to think. My thoughts were, "I am going home to stay for the first time in seven years. At twenty-four years of age I need a wife and lots of children like those I adored in England."

I stopped in Provo and found my athletic brother, Dave, and his wife, Karen, bowling. He encouraged me to come and live with them. My purpose in accepting their invitation was to spend spring quarter at the "Y" to find "the one."

There was no "mighty prayer" as I called home, disappointing my parents by telling them I wanted more credits toward a teaching credential. I dated as much as possible in my crash program of seeking a marriage partner. Rushing the normal process was doomed to failure along with my hurting—and being hurt by—a few choice young women.

The classes were too easy and for the first time in my life I was standing still, treading water, not progressing. I find too many young adults nowadays doing the same thing—wasting time while waiting for the right person to sweep them off their feet. Unhappiness flourishes with idleness. Time would be better spent with the "Pursuit of Excellence." Then they would progress and become more desirable to the opposite sex. President Kimball's instructions to young adults is for them to "decide to decide."

From intense prayer brought on by unhappiness came the answer, "Get to work, John; build for your family's future; in time you will find 'the one'; all will go well." "Seek ye first the kingdom of God, and his righteousness; and all these things shall be added unto you" (Matt. 6:33).

That summer I entered the occupation I had prepared for since high school—my father's furniture and appliance store. I also taught business subjects at Long Beach City College night school and spent every other weekend studying, in the Army reserve, psychological warfare. I was doing what inspiration directed me to do, but where was the time to date?

Five other bachelors, older than I, lived in a home near the Long Beach Stake Center. I joined them. They, too, were busy and seldom dated. Every prayer by now included a plea to find "her" soon.

From prayer came the idea which I shared with President Francis "Zip" Zimmerman of the Long Beach Stake. He had worked in our family store since its inception. He said, "Do it." Every Friday night for many years to follow there was a theme-decorated dance with large bands, mixers, entertainment, and dance contests. It was called "Friday Night in Long Beach." Average attendance the first three years was over 800 per night. M-Men and Gleaners came regularly from all over southern California.

What was the whole purpose of this effort? Originally, selfishly for myself and my roommates, to meet girls since we didn't have time to run around to other stakes. We gave away hundreds of plaques that said, "We first met at Friday Night in Long Beach." My brother Bob and his wife, Diane, got one. They met, as most, during a "mixer." After three years not one of us lonesome roommates had a glimmer of a mate.

I had another idea, probably not inspired. How about an apartment house for single Mormons? Taking my savings for a future family, I invested in a new apartment building with nine units and room to build more, in North Long Beach. (Not until I abandoned the singles idea did the investment succeed.)

Both the dance and the apartment idea helped me eventually choose my wife. There was a pretty, shapely, olive-skinned young girl who was on the dance committee as Gleaner president of the Long Beach East Stake. She was only nineteen when we first met, but we had fun together for the next two years. When she started dating one of the few single guys living in my apartments, I was agitated.

Standing at attention for flag salute at Fort MacArthur, San Pedro, overlooking the misty Pacific Ocean at 6:00 a.m. on a Sunday morning, I said to myself, "What are you doing here when you should be taking your own family, if you had one, to church?" I went AWOL to my empty apartment and began to plead to God on my knees for the umpteenth time to find her now. I could visualize "postponing the responsibilities of life" my patriarchal blessing warned me against. This prayer was as intense as another I had offered two years earlier when I begged the Lord to let my next date be the "right one."

I would have prayed longer, but I needed to prepare for a fireside talk in Hollywood that evening. As I prepared, there came an overpowering feeling within me and in the room similar to my experience in the bathroom in London. I noted the answer to my prayer as it unfolded in my mind. The pages became wet as I wrote, "You dummy, Sondra Pinegar was placed in your arms two years ago after you last poured out your heart on this matter. Sure she's young, although she's twenty-one now. You've been with her at Friday night dances and committee meetings for two years. You've enjoyed every date and shared all your feelings with her. She's even helped clean the apartments. She has been in love with you for a year and you have hurt her at times by wavering. Come on, John, do you love her? Would she be a good mother to your children? What's this nonsense about waiting for her missionary to return from England? You say you didn't want him hurt or pining away after Sondra: excuses, excuses! He's been home a whole week now. You are twenty-eight and should have been engaged to Sondra a year ago. Sure it was necessary to have the frustration of unknowingly waiting for her to mature. You may have waited too long. She has other interests. Act now!" This may not sound like revelation — it was to me.

While the Spirit of the Lord lingered, I wrote Sondra a letter of proposal. Then I rushed to give a shortened fireside. When I drove to Sondra's house later that evening her younger sister, Linda, told me that Sondra was out with my tenant. I fell asleep on the living room couch waiting for her late return. When they drove up, Linda ran out and told Sondra — just as my tenant was working up to kissing her for the first time — "John's in there!" When she came in she read my proposal. We both fought back the tears of joy as Sondra said "Yes." I promptly went home, thanked the Lord, and suggested strongly to the tenant that he find housing elsewhere.

We were married in the Los Angeles Temple on March 16, 1963. Sondra, attired in white, radiated a heavenly beauty as we held hands across the altar of the celestial sealing room. I had found my eternal date. After years of frustrated seeking, I was now a husband and although I was unaware of it at the time, I was also a patriarch in my home.

I was unable to attend the wedding years later of Shelly Hatch and John Fishbien. They received my telegram as they came out of the sealing room of the Los Angeles Temple. They read: "Congratulations on your marriage to the right person, in the right place, at the right time."

Some young adults miss on all three counts. Many miss "the right time" by not putting forth the effort to actively seek, prepare themselves, pray, or recognize the answer to prayer. I probably should have married Sondra a year earlier.

Temple Marriage

With the knowledge of being married to "the one" that God inspired you to select, it is only natural that you will want to give blessings to your wife and children. You have in common a testimony of Christ, the restoration, temple sealings, and priesthood authority. Righteous courtship insures inspiration for a "marriage made in heaven." In an eternal family, blessings are given as often as they are needed. All couples should progress step-by-step toward eternal marriage, then continue to progress toward exaltation. Blessings become more a part of our lives as we progress.

A very nice, athletic young man was playing on our ward basketball team. His girlfriend was a Laurel. Although he was not a member of the Church, he asked me to give him a blessing before he went to Vietnam with the Army. On his return, he asked me to marry them. We had some good talks in the bishop's office. Before I married them in the chapel, I fasted and prayed that the ceremony would be special for this exceptional young couple, and it was a spiritual occasion, tastefully done.

Afterward a Mia Maid girl said, "Bishop, someday I want you to perform my marriage ceremony." I said, "You want to be married for eternity in the temple. I'm sorry, but I can only marry a couple for time, till death do they part."

I married another couple a few months later. This ceremony was vastly different! The feuding family met on neutral ground at a local community church where I participated with another minister in marrying them. The vulgar talk of the groom's entourage prior to the ceremony, the rush forced on us by others waiting to be married, the paid singers and preacher and— worst of all—our uninspired words were a sacrilege. The civil wedding was, however, valid even to God.

At a fireside the following Sunday, I told the youth that I, as bishop, would not marry anyone again because it meant a non-temple marriage. Well, I did marry a few more couples, but most of the youth at the fireside were married in the temple. The Lord's spirit is in the House of the Lord. So is the authority to bind on earth and in heaven for eternity.

My wife and I took four newly engaged Young Adult couples out to our favorite restaurant. One member in each couple was a recent convert. All were Young Adult leaders planning a near-future temple marriage. It was a good-looking group that shared, during dinner, how they met, proposed, and how they knew they had found "the one." With other diners listening attentively, we laughed and shared testimonies. During their courtship, each of these young people received personal revelation concerning their "intended" after fasting and prayer. It must have been strange conversation to intrigued diners and waitresses nearby.

A year later, these devoted couples joined us for dinner at our home. The converts shed tears for what the gospel had meant to them. Each one knows their mate selection was inspired and that there is a true patriarch in their home.

Inspiration for Business

God's help is not confined just to personal, family, and church matters. Many times I have sought His help in business matters. Our store joined a newly formed group of television and appliance dealers in 1972. Associated Volume Buyers (AVB) was originally formed to combat the advantage large chain stores have of buying in volume. Independent dealers are just that— independent. Our board meetings included shouting matches, occasional drunkenness, and even one occasion when a fist-fight took place. We were trying to cater to dealers with annual sales from $300,000 to $30 million. We needed to overcome our problems or be gobbled up by the chains. Yet, after two years, our bylaws were still unsettled.

I contrasted this setting with the high council meetings I attended. These high councilors were also strong-willed and different in their personalities, but every decision which came from this church "board of directors" was unanimous.

At one AVB meeting during the height of discord, the group's president resigned. A meeting of board members was hurriedly called. I prayed for strength before attending what I knew would be a donnybrook. One energetic board member, seeking to be president, represented a growing feeling among our now eighty-three stores: "Only large dealers should be allowed to join. Only approved brands should be sold. All stores should conform or leave the group. There should be more power in the presidency and fewer board members. Dealers would give up independence, but be guaranteed a profit . . ."

As heads began to nod affirmatively, I stood and said, "What I have heard would split the group into factions worse than we have now. We should continue to grow and to take in all honest dealers, large and small. Every dealer should be allowed his agency in deciding brands, promotions, and store policies. In time, the members will follow the board's lead if our ideas are successful. Every member should have a position on numerous committees. This board needs to stop its feuding and become an example for the members to follow."

I said a lot more, with emotion, emphasizing the need for unity. Afterwards, no one else spoke. Normally everyone would have given their "two-cents worth." Then our founder said, "I nominate John Ward to be president." My protesting was weak since I felt that it was right. On the way home that night I realized that a plan of free agency had won out over a plan of force, and I gave thanks.

At the following AVB general meeting I put forth a much prayed-about plan of unity, agency, and growth. I also told board members that my family, church, and store came first with me and that at times the board would be inconvenienced. Even so, the vote to sustain me as president was unanimous. AVB now has over 500 stores in eight states with over $500 million in sales. It is the largest association of its kind in the world.

Would God have interceded to answer my prayer thus helping other independent businessmen? I believe so. The principles of the gospel are not limited just to individuals and church. We need his blessings in our work, too.

Weekly, early-morning Monday sales meetings, and all of our store's board meetings are opened with prayer. Various manufacturer's representatives who attend our sales meetings seem to appreciate the divine assistance asked for on their behalf. The frequent repetitious prayer of being honest in all our dealings with customers has made our store successful with a very high return patronage.

Repentance

When we have developed a relationship with our Heavenly Father through "mighty prayer" and followed His commandments, we can anticipate His influence and forgiveness. As we fail in this relationship, we lose precious time. All that is needed is for us to repent, to get back on the "straight and narrow," and to feel again his blessings poured out upon us.

My first interview as a bishop concerning transgression was with a despondent teen-age girl who had really messed up her life. I was not sure how to help. She was trapped hopelessly in a "Catch 22" situation. My counselor and I gave her a blessing.

Later, as I was driving home, I pulled the car over to fight the welling up of sorrow within me. The injustice of the girl's problems, and the severe consequences of passion-caused immoral acts, were heavy to bear. Where were the father and mother in her time of need? What was I to do? Helpless, I prayed. Immediately came a calm peace as I remembered the scripture: "For I the Lord cannot look upon sin with the least degree of allowance; nevertheless, he that repents and does the commandments of the Lord shall be forgiven" (D&C 1:31-32).

The next Sunday her sobbing words spoke of her love of the Savior, her sorrow, and of her desire to do the will of her Heavenly Father. I learned the significance of Christ's atonement, the meaning of repentance and complete forgiveness because of this young girl's repentance.

Our Heavenly Father truly answers our humble prayers. He blesses us throughout life. There may be no need for a priesthood blessing in many instances; only God's inspiration is necessary. Why, then, do men called of God lay hands on a person's head? A lengthy answer could be given dealing with priesthood authority, but answered simply: our Father has authorized priesthood blessings to help his children in all facets of their lives.

Blessings from Priesthood Leadership

Setting a person apart to a position, conferring the priesthood, and ordaining to an office within the priesthood are common forms of priesthood leadership blessings. A worthy father is usually asked to perform some of these ordinations in behalf of his children.

Setting Apart and Ordinations

During my second year as bishop, from June to September, 122 people were called and set apart to new positions. This re-shuffling included almost all youth and adult positions. Groups within organizations would meet after sacrament meeting in the Relief Society room to be set apart and blessed by my counselors and me. These were spiritual events where individuals not only received inspiration to their new calling but, in many cases, new insight about themselves, families, and friends. Health, foreordination, study, occupation, marriage, and many other subjects were mentioned in these inspired blessings.

One evening as we walked back to the bishop's office, my counselor, Nils Johansen, said, "Do you remember telling Sister Jackson that she would join the Church soon because of the actions of the youth?" We had just set her apart as second counselor in the Young Women's organization.

Her daughter had joined the Church a few months earlier. Sister Jackson, a capable community leader, had shown an interest in MIA activities but not Church doctrine. A few weeks later she helped chaperon an exciting trip to Salt Lake City for ninety-two of our youth.

Our final meeting was held in BYU's Helaman Halls. As all of us knelt in prayer, Sister Jackson said, "Bishop, excuse me, before we pray I'd like to say something." She paused, wiped her eyes, and spoke haltingly with emotion. "This week has been memorable. I've seen your temple, met your apostles, but the reason I know your Church is true is because of the actions and testimonies of the youth kneeling here. I want to be baptized!"

We may be apprehensive when we are set apart to a new position but the Lord surely helps us if we put forth the effort. Listen carefully when you are being set apart. The Lord talks to us through his priesthood mouthpiece. If too much time has passed since you were called to a position and you have not been set apart, do not hesitate to contact the appropriate priesthood leader. Sometimes it helps to remind them of the need for further inspiration.

After I spoke about blessings at a regional Young Adult fireside in Whittier, California, a sister came up to me and sounding frustrated said, "I've never been set apart to my Relief Society calling. Would you please do it?" I smiled and said, "Besides the Melchizedek Priesthood I must have the proper keys to set you apart. Ask your bishop; he'll be glad to see that you are set apart. Just ask."

Some church callings or assignments may not specifically require a setting apart. However, a member may request to be set apart. In nearly all cases a request will be welcomed.

Conferring the Aaronic Priesthood and ordaining to the office of deacon, teacher, or priest is by direction of the bishop. Conferring the Melchizedek Priesthood and ordaining to the office of elder, seventy, or high priest is by the direction of the stake president. So far, at the request of my sons, I've been directed by the presiding authority to confer the priesthood and ordain them. My sons who are priests and elders have assisted me with the ordaining of their younger brothers. These are special family and quorum occasions. Where there is not a father in the home, a relative, home teacher, or other priesthood leader may be directed to give these ordinations.

For example, my sons went to Provo to participate in the ordination of their cousin, Todd, a deacon. Sometimes priesthood bearers must assume what is usually a father's privilege, in his absence, to give a child a name and a blessing, baptize, confirm, and give other special blessings.

Only the baptismal, sacrament, and temple ordinance prayers must be word-perfect. A few key phrases should be mentioned in all other forms of blessings. These are reviewed in quorum meetings. The procedures to follow are simple. Some seem to make giving a blessing difficult, such as when two large elders with massive hands try to get all their fingers on an infant's small head.

Blessings from a Judge in Israel

One afternoon a youth leader was sharing his patriarchal blessing with me in the bishop's office. Although he didn't understand some of the terminology his was a marvelous blessing. He had tilted his chair back waiting for me to finish my engrossed reading of it. He could wait no longer and finally blurted out, "What does it mean I'll be 'a judge in Israel'?" When I responded "It means someday you can be a bishop," he tipped over backward.

A father can turn to his bishop for help in making judgments. He should encourage members of his family to seek out the bishop. Locally only the bishop and stake president can judge the full repentance of grievous sins.

It's hard for me to imagine a successful father/patriarch or wife/mother who do not have the help of a good bishop. As a lay minister, a bishop spends so much time with the youth that his influence is a great force in their lives. Favorable comments about the bishop during family discussions and prayers encourage our children to seek him out when they are troubled.

I'll never forget an event that took place a month after I was made bishop. A youth came to MIA with "pills." Our youth council after lengthy, serious discussion decided that drugs were not going to be available to their younger brothers and sisters. One youth confessed his involvement. Within a few weeks, seven of our youth were given the choice of telling their parents of their involvement or having me tell them.

Rumor and gossip concerning this incident were destructive to the ward. I notified adjoining ward bishops of youth in their wards who had been implicated. As the whirlwind of rumor and gossip continued among the adults, every youth who experimented with drugs was repenting. Never again would drugs be a problem in the Lakewood Second Ward, except for a few isolated incidents. My problem now was with parents who over-reacted, were embarrassed, or who criticized me. One parent said to his son, "Bishop Ward doesn't know what he's talking about." I was never able to fully help that young man, no matter how hard I tried.

During youth week the youth held every ward position. The youth choir, consisting of ninety-two youths, was directed by talented Lynn Venuti, who had never led music. The youth choir was invited to sing at our stake conference, and sixteen-year-old Lynn was told at the last minute that she was also expected to direct the congregational singing. This, too, she had never done. She said to me, "Bishop, will you please give me a blessing? I know it will help." Five minutes after I laid my hands on her head she expertly and enthusiastically directed the singing. The compliments to her and the youth choir were superlative.

Would Lynn have asked for a blessing if her parents had expressed doubts about the bishop? Do we ask blessings of our father/patriarch if we have doubts about him or if he lacks faith in himself?

After a particularly busy three months, I made a list of problems the Lord had inspired me, as a young bishop, to handle: runaway youths, foster care placement, desertion of mission, desecration of flag, involvement with witchcraft, fornication, common-law marriage, adultery, attempted suicide, abortion, family desertion, attempted murder, draft evasion, AWOL, incest, drug abuse, drug addiction, alcoholism, divorce, annulment, child abuse, larceny, violation of parole, deep depression, venereal disease, homosexuality, disfellowshipment, and excommunication.

In most of these cases there was not an active priesthood bearer in the home. In a few, the father/patriarch and I counseled together before or after my assistance to the family member. I was careful not to reveal confidential information.

Most of the people with these problems repented. A few became even worse off. I felt love for all of them. I learned that active church families have problems too, but inactive families seem to have the gigantic problems which last longer. The closer the parents are to their God and the bishop, the quicker the problem is resolved through repentance and the Lord's forgiveness. It is good for me to know that there is a bishop, a "judge in Israel," who loves my wife, my children, and me. He is someone on earth to talk to who will not reveal a confidence.

A choice young couple came to the bishop's office seeking help. They had been married for several years and their doctor had told them they would never be able to have children. They shared their patriarchal blessings with me—blessings which said they would "raise many children." As we talked I felt prompted to suggest that they each receive a blessing. "We hoped you would give us a blessing," they seemed relieved to say.

First I laid hands on the husband's head, then he assisted me in blessing his wife. I spoke the words that came to me from the Lord: "You shall have many children, beginning soon." About nine months later they had their first child. Even after they moved out of my ward, they still called at the birth of each new child.

I will never forget the blessing my bishop gave me shortly after my mission. A scholarship had been granted to me for New York University's School of Retailing a month before I left England. I arrived from my mission by plane at gigantic LaGuardia Airport. Since I had no place to live I looked up the bishop's phone number to ask him for help. To my relief, the bishop of the Manhattan Ward, Grant Bethers, was single and looking for another roommate. He found me.

I settled into intense study so that I could obtain my Master of Science degree in retailing in nine months. When I was called to be a counselor in the ward genealogy presidency, I was dumbfounded. I had not done any genealogy and I had no interest in it. I was a hard-pressed student who had just begun a part-time job.

It was obvious to my gentle, compassionate roommate that I was upset. He suggested a blessing. I was promised that if I accepted this calling, and others that would follow, I would "excel" in my school work. Other promises were given but that one stood out. Two other callings followed: genealogy class teacher and genealogy stake board. These assignments took me throughout New York, Connecticut, and New Jersey. My busy school year ended with several awards, job offers and straight A's. Credit for this year in which I surpassed my own ability goes to my bishop and my God.

The bishop's responsibility is primarily to the youth. He is especially watchful when there is not significant parental support at home. Sometimes he might seek a youth out for counseling, especially if there is not a father or an active mother in the home.

A teacher, while visiting one of her Mia Maids, was shocked at the gloomy pictures on the teenager's wildly colored bedroom walls. She felt what she described as an "evil spirit" in the room. The girl was well-known to me. She had joined the Church the year before, but she had continued her friendship with drug-oriented schoolmates. The temptations had been too subtle and constant for her to resist. In previous interviews, and at youth activities, we had gained respect for each other.

Reluctantly, at my request, she came to see me. It was obvious from her obscene language and torrid demeanor that she was not only on drugs, but also possessed. My counselor and I laid our hands on her twisting head and commanded the evil spirit to leave in the name of Jesus Christ. As the spirit left screaming, the youth slumped off her chair to the floor. Her mother took her home and the next day she was happy and resolved to change her life—beginning with her "friends." Even when she was possessed, the respect we had developed for each other overcame her reluctance to see the bishop.

A father/patriarch could have cast out that evil spirit. There is nothing special about the bishop doing it. Any righteous Melchizedek priesthood bearer by the power of the priesthood can command any evil presence to depart. There is no formal procedure to follow other than the statement of authority and "In the name of Jesus Christ."

After the birth of our second child, Sondra entered a "blue period." I didn't understand what was happening and I was not very supportive. One night I was kept awake by her tossing and turning. I sat upright at her first scream.

"What's wrong?" I stammered.

"Make it go away, make it go away," she pleaded.

"Make *what* go away?" I asked uneasily.

"That," she gasped, pointing to the foot of the bed.

I had encountered evil forces of the unseen world in the mission field. I could recognize them and I knew what to do. Hugging Sondra, I spoke clearly and powerfully: "In the name of Jesus Christ and by authority of the Holy Melchizedek Priesthood, I command the evil spirit present to depart." Immediately, a cat in our front yard went beserk, with sustained, screeching "meows."

Sondra and I held each other tightly. I got up to make sure the children were all right while the cat continued the shuddering cries. They were peacefully asleep, as they should be, since Satan has no influence over little children (D&C 29).

The next morning we found cat hair all over our lawn, bushes, and a tree trunk. I told President Zimmerman, Long Beach stake president, at our store what had taken place. After work he came to our home and talked to us about what had happened. The stake president is also a judge in Israel. At our request, he gave troubled Sondra a blessing with my assistance. His inspired words gave us insight into her "blue period" and the night of fright. She was told of the great love the Lord had for her and the reasons for her depression. President Zimmerman said that significant good would come from the experience. Sondra recovered quickly; we learned much, and we have not had another sinister experience in our more than twenty years of marriage. The experience helped us both to assist others.

Church members should not be reluctant to ask for a blessing when they are inspired to do so. If not father, then home teacher; if he has not visited lately, there is the quorum president and always the ever-busy bishop. In fact, any Melchizedek Priesthood bearer can give a blessing. There is no "chain of command" or restrictions to ward or stake. We should look first to those closest to us who have stewardship for us. If they are reluctant, unworthy, or unavailable, any worthy elder may be asked. Do not suffer longer than is necessary because you lack ready access to a priesthood blessing.

Blessings from the Home Teacher

Our junior basketball team was tied going into the final minutes of the game. Mike, our quick forward, drove in for a lay-up. He was fouled and he came down full-weight in an awkward position on his right foot. Those present could hear the crack of breaking bone. Mike was going into shock and he asked his coach for a blessing.

Early the next morning I was notified. As Mike's home teacher I rushed to the hospital. His mother was there. She was a worried single parent for the prognosis was alarming. Mike had shattered bones in his foot and ankle. They would take a long time to heal and it was doubtful that Mike would ever play ball again. Such news would be difficult to handle at any age. For one who was a teenager, and for whom sports were a vital part of life, the news was devastating. After I was shown the X-rays of what looked like dozens of bone particles scattered in Mike's foot, I went to see him.

I asked, "Mike, do you remember the blessing you received lying on the gym floor?" He paused, then said groggily, "A little bit." "Will you get better?" I asked. "I think so," he replied weakly. We talked about accidents, tragedies, and blessings. "Now that you know about your condition, would you like a confirming blessing?" I was impressed to ask.

I was apprehensive afterwards at the words spoken: "You will completely recover! You will play ball next season! This will be a good learning experience for you. Do your school work . . ."

Shortly after that Mike's family moved. The next spring our Young Adult basketball team had reached the final game of the area playoffs. I do not remember whether or not we won. I do remember having a big trophy shoved in my lap as I sat in the bleachers waiting for our game to start.

"What is this?" I said to the sweating uniformed youth who had plopped down beside me. Then, jubilant in recognition, I said, "Mike! How the heck are you?"

He pointed at his foot and then at the trophy and said, "Read it." The inscription on the trophy stood out . . . "Area Junior Basketball Most Outstanding Player." He had been awarded the trophy ten minutes earlier.

Our family has had the same home teacher for many years. We certainly have faith and love for "Big Jim" Dunlap and his lovely wife, Beverly. Admittedly, he doesn't always make monthly housecalls. He is ever present when needed, though. In participating in some of our family mishaps he has said, "I've got enough home teaching in during this week to last me the rest of the year."

One Easter vacation we loaded up the van, motor home, and trailer with our nine children, six dirt bikes, and the two older sons' girlfriends. This was the first time they had dated these girls and we were going to the sand dunes southeast of the Salton Sea for a week's vacation. Before we left, the parents of the girls joined us as we prayed for a "serious accident-free trip."

Our home teacher and his wife met us in the desert along with other friends from our ward. "Old Yella," the Dunlap's dune buggy, took our family up, down and around the huge sand dunes. Nothing but sand and sky could be seen for miles.

Our four red Honda two-wheel dirt bikes had to keep moving to stay on top of the sand. If we stopped it was usually when we were heading downhill. The Honda three-wheel ATC's (All Terrain Cycles) could go almost anywhere but they had a tendency to roll if a hilly dune was attacked too slowly. Rolling, falling and crashing in protective soft sand is part of our favorite vacation. Playing "follow-the-leader" around the tall sagebrush by the All-American Canal is great fun. With protective clothing and helmets, the minor injuries were attended to by retired fire chief "Big Jim" or by one of our paramedic friends camped nearby.

Sondra is a professional photographer and she finds the dunes and sunsets irresistible. As twilight came, Sondra, with Lesa on her three-wheeler, sought to find a deserted spot where she could photograph the lengthening shadows. Joey followed on the other three-wheeler while I brought up the rear on my two-wheel dirt bike. Since I could not stop in some of the places

Sondra chose to photograph, I would zoom around inside the dune bowls using centrifugal force to lift me up from the bottom.

We all stopped on a high sand dune and I indicated we had better start back before dark. Since I was sinking in the sand, I took off as Sondra finished a series of pictures. As I came back later, I shouted, "Where's Joey?" "He followed you!" she responded. I back-tracked and found fourteen-year-old Joey at the bottom of a dune bowl motionless and face down in the sand. His three-wheeler was lying upside-down a few yards away. I sped down the dune, dropped my bike and asked, knowing the answer, "Joey, are you all right?" He gasped, "No, I can't move." I turned his head gently and wiped the sand out of his eyes, nose, and mouth. As I examined him, he began to cry softly and asked for a blessing. I did not remove his helmet. With my hands on his sandy cheeks, I prayed fervently for my son. By now, surely Sondra would have guessed something was amiss. Where was she?

She had become worried when we did not return right away and she wondered if my shouted instructions over the roar of motorcycle engines had meant for them to head for camp, and that I would return with Joey. She was apprehensive about finding her way out of the dunes. She began to look for the road or a canal so she could get her bearings.

As darkness fell the wind began to blow showering particles of sand over the dune's crest. Joey was in shock. It took a while for me to get his flooded three-wheeler started. I drove it to the top of a big dune where its silhouette could be seen for a mile. The nagging realization that I might not be able to find this place again, day or night, was a haunting reality. Perhaps some night-riding dune buggies would sight the three-wheeler. I rushed back down, plowing deep furrows in the sand, to where Joey lay as though he were dead.

In my panic not only had I flooded my bike when I dropped it, I had stopped at the bottom of the deep dune bowl. The blessing I had given Joey had said that he would be all right. That thought sustained me as the bike finally kicked over. I looked at Joey and saw in his tearful eyes a look of quiet desperation. "I love you, Joey, I'll be back soon!" I shouted as I shot up out of the dune heading toward where I thought the sun had set. Fortunately my bike had a light. I prayed for help as I went up and down dune after dune. Twenty minutes later I had ridden straight to camp getting there just as Sondra and Lesa arrived.

The cry was repeated several times: "Joey's down!" Several dune buggies "fired up" and leading the search I was off. I had noted a few reference points and now I found them in the moonlight. My own tracks were nearly obliterated by the blowing sand.

The high beams of the dune buggies lit up the sand and sky as we roared across the once-still desert. Then we saw the ATC silhouetted against the moon-lit sky.

Joey was partially covered with sand but still conscious. The firemen guessed he had a broken leg above the knee. We knew that the pain for Joey was awful as the firemen applied a cardboard splint. The pain was obviously even worse as they lifted him into the cramped back bucket-seats of a dune buggy. His leg was being held outside the buggy in front of the giant rear sand tire. I could hear Joey's moans as I followed the bouncing dune buggy. I watched his helmeted head occasionally bounce off the tire on the other side.

Those who had gone ahead found a 4-by-4 truck owned by a stranger who was willing to help. As they transferred Joey I raced to camp to get our van. This time I got lost. After crashing through bushes I finally got up on the bank of the canal and saw the camp fires. Driving the van fast over the rutted canal road was folly but I got to the road's end just as the 4-by-4 arrived with Joey.

As Sondra comforted Joey and kept him warm in the rear of the van, "Big Jim" gave me directions to the hospital in Brawley, twenty miles away. "Don't worry about your family," he said. I hadn't even thought about them but I did as I drove. I prayed for Joey and gave thanks for my home teacher.

Seeing Joey's X-ray made us gasp. He had broken the biggest bone in his body, the femur at the top part of his left leg. The sharpness of the bone and the distance between the two pieces was sickening. It appeared that as Joey had followed me down the dune he had hit a bump which threw him over the handlebars. The three-wheeler had gone up and then down with a handlebar landing squarely on Joey's leg.

The bottle of consecrated oil in my pocket had somehow been acquired during the frenzy. Joey was sedated but alert. "Let's do the blessing again with oil, Joey," I said. I anointed, then sealed the anointing, blessing him again that he would recover quickly. (Could this be possible?)

Joey was transferred to El Centro Hospital where he was in surgery for what seemed like all day. An eight-inch metal plate, two pins and ten screws along with two blood transfusions put him together again. The Dunlaps took care of the family in camp while Sondra and I were with Joey.

Michael stopped his cycle distance-jumping and everyone wore the proper safety equipment. Camp was subdued but everyone was having fun—even Big Jim. When Lindsay came down with chicken pox two days later, Jim anointed and I blessed her. "Enough!" we thought. Jim and Beverly volunteered to take the little children and follow our teenagers and their dates home. A few days later we took Joey in the motor home to the Long Beach Memorial Medical Center.

After a visit to Joey, I asked our home teacher if he would drop by the house. We lined up four more children with chicken pox and administered to them and their fatigued mother. As he left Jim winked and said, "I'll never camp with you guys again."

Joey returned to junior high school on crutches the following week. When we were making out his schedule for his sophomore year we originally opted for remedial physical education, but his leg healed so well the doctor allowed him to sign up for water polo. Four months after his accident he was on the water polo team where he lettered. In that year he grew three inches with no limp. He also had lots of loving attention which is exactly what he needed at this time in his life. Joey gives credit to his Heavenly Father, the power of the priesthood, Big Jim, his own faith and hard work and his parents for his recovery. It all came together to help one frightened young boy alone on the desert sand.

Patriarchal Blessings

All worthy church members should receive a recorded patriarchal blessing from their stake patriarch. In that priesthood blessing a declaration of our lineage and foreordained mission is given along with warnings and admonitions. Promises by the Lord are made which are conditioned upon faithfulness.

Confidence Gained from Patriarchal Blessings

At age fifteen, I was taken by my parents to receive my patriarchal blessing from J. Roland Sandstrom. I found it difficult to believe or understand much of what the patriarch said in my blessing. How could a shy, short, skinny boy do all that was promised to him. I was struggling with schoolwork, I was chosen near the last for sports teams, I had few friends, and I slumped with my eyes down from lack of self-confidence. When the written blessing came in the mail it confirmed all that had been spoken. My parents believed it. My doubts remained secret. Quite often I would peek at my blessing to see if the promises were still there.

By the middle of my junior year in high school this "late learner" began to come out of his shell. Grades improved, I made the "B" basketball team and I bought freedom in a 1942 Chevrolet Club Coupe by working in the family store after school.

My first date was a disaster and contributed to my bashfulness. My mother and the mayor's wife thought it would be splendid if their children met. I was sixteen, she was fourteen. I had been invited to the mayor's house for dinner. My mother diligently coached me on table manners. As I walked up the path to the Corinthian-columned colonial home, my knees buckled.

Paula's family was very nice to me as we sat down for dinner. I held Paula's chair as I had rehearsed with Mom. I observed the eating motions of the person opposite me. When she drank, I drank. Unfortunately the water "went down the wrong throat." About the time I began to slide under the table from embarrassed coughing Paula's elegant mother took me into the kitchen until I recovered. I ate little and drank nothing more during the meal.

My mother was waiting in the car to take us to the new Crest Theater in Long Beach. As I had carefully rehearsed, I opened the car door for Paula. She gave me a funny look and got in the front seat. Since that didn't leave enough room for me in the front seat I opened the rear door and got in the back seat.

As we watched the movie I tried to make conversation. Paula never acknowledged my comments. I thought she was mad at me. Later I learned she was hard-of-hearing in the ear into which I was whispering. When we were leaving the theatre some of Paula's friends watched us and snickered. There was Mother to pick us up. It was raining. The theater's multi-colored sidewalk was slick. This time I opened the car's rear door. As I pulled on the heavy door my feet slipped and I fell underneath the car and into the gutter. Mom took me home first since I was all wet.

I was a klutz and I knew it. How could the patriarch describe me differently in my blessing. Even as I gained confidence in my senior year I was blackballed from a fraternity, I lost my first election and I ate lunch alone.

Entering and knowing only one person at BYU was very awkward, yet my confidence was growing. The first Sunday I attended the BYU branch that was held in the Joseph Smith Auditorium. I was sitting on the stage in front of one of the sacrament tables and I was extremely self-conscious. Some twenty of us were to pass the sacrament to an overflow congregation of peers. The immaculate surroundings of freshly painted walls, newly waxed floors and beautifully dressed girls made me think of my grooming. My hair was combed and I had on my new suit and shoes. Yes, college was a new beginning for me.

As I passed the bread I was more aware of my surroundings than I was of the holy sacrament. Then it happened! When I went down the stage steps carrying two sacrament trays of water-filled cups, my new shoes hit the newly waxed floor. My feet shot out from under me and I fell flat on my back with arms extended, the trays overhead. Water and cups spilled all over me. A few years earlier, my BYU studies would have ended at that very moment. Even with the God-given growth in my confidence it was fortunate that I was not asked to pass the sacrament again for several months.

While I was attending my first Recreation Commission Meeting my former basketball coach, Del Walker, Chairman of the Commission, introduced me and told this story: "We were playing Jordon High School in their gym for the league championship. With seconds left and the game tied our star player fouled out on a double foul. The opponent missed his free throw and I sent John in because he was the best free-throw shooter. As the packed gym went wild John bounced the ball several times, took deliberate aim, and shot. Not only did he miss the basket, he missed the backboard, rim and net by five feet! During the next playoff game I said, 'Ward, go in for Stanfield.' John knelt down by me and said, 'Gee coach, don't you want to win the game?' "

By the time high school graduation came my blessing was a reality embedded in my goals. The shy boy who seldom talked to people blossomed as the blessing promised. Even though I ran for freshman president at BYU and lost, I wanted to "develop the ability to serve" as I had been instructed in the blessing so I ran for sophomore president and won. The year I became student body second vice-president my brother, David, became sophomore president. BYU's yearbook has a "Banyon Personality" section for which I was selected four straight years. During most of my youth I knew I had no personality and even with the seeming success at BYU, I still was not sure of myself. I was, however, trying hard to fulfill my blessing.

Some people in community associations remember me from my junior high and high school days. They say they can't believe the change; nor at times can I. I still slip away from groups of people unless I am in some way responsible for the gathering.

I have witnessed many youth and young adults suffer through their school years from a lack of self-confidence. Many give up. They may think they are dumb so they don't study. They have no friends so they do not talk to anyone. They think their appearance is a mess so they dress accordingly. They feel uncoordinated so they don't join teams. In time they become what they imagine themselves to be. I know! In the depths of sorrow for what I felt to be my lack of personality I might have given up if I had not been given divine insight into what God wanted me to do.

I have great empathy for the loser. I usually root for the underdog or the losing team. I know that losers can become winners. They only need to gain confidence by working harder. From my early teens I acquired a sensitivity to all categories of people.

A patriarchal blessing lifted me up and put me on my way to becoming a happy human being and a profitable servant of God. Parents should tactfully suggest to their children a patriarchal blessing when they are mature enough to understand its meaning, usually at about age sixteen.

Interpretation of Patriarchal Blessings

At a youth fireside shortly after I became bishop, Long Beach East Stake's new patriarch, Theodore P. Malquist, gave an inspirational talk. The question was asked, "Who may read a patriarchal blessing?" The patriarch said, "Your blessing is sacred and should not be indiscriminately shared with friends. Where appropriate, your current and future family may read it. If you have questions about your blessing come see me or share it with your bishop."

That comment resulted in many of the youth in the ward sharing their private blessing with me while I was their bishop. During the recommend interview for a patriarchal blessing I would conclude with, "You may have questions about your blessing so please don't hesitate to see me." These shared times were memorable, spiritual moments in my life. The youth would enter the bishop's office enthusiastic and proud about the words inside the outstretched envelope. I would caution them that only they, not me, could interpret, with the Lord's help, the meaning of the rendered blessing. (After reading my patriarchal blessing over a hundred times there still remains new insight when it is needed.)

The youth and I would kneel and ask for the Lord's spirit to be with us. As a few lines were read aloud a smile from me would help the youth know that their bishop knew they would accomplish all they had been foreordained to do. We usually talked about some of the warnings.

I knew the truth of my blessing and, during this period of sharing, my testimony of patriarchal blessings in general was amplified. Patriarch Malquist only casually (if at all) knew these youth. I knew them well. In every case the blessings were different and each one seemed to fit the individual I knew. Of course there were plenty of surprises—happy surprises. There were some similarities since most of our pre-existence and eternal goals are the same. This sharing was a special time in their life and in mine.

A young woman who was married to a non-member came to me, as her bishop, for counseling. I was impressed with her talents and potential for accomplishing great things in her life. My impression was verified in a second visit when she shared her patriarchal blessing with me. She said, "I have lost faith in my blessing. Most of the things promised to me have not come to pass." "Why not?" I asked. She answered correctly, "Well, maybe I wasn't living right at the time when I was supposed to do the things I was promised." We determined that most of the blessings promised her could still take place. She had lost time, but with repentance and an extra degree of effort she could still fulfill her foreordained life.

If a patriarchal blessing says "temple marriage," can not a person postpone a civil marriage until the temple marriage is possible either by repentance or conversion? Those who follow lives contrary to their patriarchal blessing jeopardize their exaltation by not following God's will.

While we were setting future goals my wife said, "My patriarchal blessing appears to have concluded when I got married." I agreed. Most of her relatively short blessing, obtained when she was sixteen years of age, dealt with her teen-age and young-adult years. She decided I might be prejudiced as her bishop so she sought out the stake patriarch. He gave her a long, beautiful continuation to her original blessing.

Here was new information about raising a large family and pursuing her talents. Knowing God's will, she was again fortified concerning her future. A continuation patriarchal blessing is uncommon and usually not necessary or recommended. Special blessings given by the husband or another priesthood bearer can give added insight into one's life. After such blessings it is helpful to write down remembered divine direction.

A patriarchal blessing from the stake patriarch is recorded, transcribed, and a copy is kept in the Church offices in Salt Lake City. If your copy is lost it may be replaced by contacting the Church offices. A patriarchal blessing given by a father to his children may be recorded and kept in a family Book of Remembrance. A copy of the father's blessing is not kept in the Church offices.

Blessings given to us for different reasons by all priesthood bearers give us comfort and direction. Remember, God's revelation to us is not a one-time event. It should be a lifelong pursuit.

III

Giving Blessings More Often

Generally speaking, blessings need to be given more often. Very few people ask too frequently. Many church members hesitate too long before they ask. It may be appropriate, in some instances, to suggest that a person ask for a blessing. A father might say to a child, "When you feel like it, don't forget to ask Daddy for a blessing to help you get over that cold." We assume children and adults will ask for blessings when they are ready, but either they do not know how to or they are reluctant to impose.

Questions About Blessings

For a while the high council and stake presidency of the Long Beach East Stake were meeting once a month to study a gospel topic. These were spiritually enlightening gatherings for all of us as we attempted to become one in thought and deed.

When my turn came to present the lesson I was assigned the subject "Healing of the Sick." I studied everything available to me. My studies raised even more questions about the giving of blessings than I started with, so instead of giving a lecture I prepared the following questions:

1. What kinds of blessings by the laying on of hands can a father give his family?

2. Is it always necessary for two elders to bless the sick?

3. May a non-member or woman join in the laying on of hands to bless the sick?

4. Can the sick be blessed without anointing with oil?

5. Must a person ask for a blessing before it can be given?

6. How sick should we be before we call the elders?

7. Are repeated anointings to an individual necessary?

8. Is it proper to "dedicate to the Lord" the very sick?

9. Are a person's sins forgiven when they are healed as stated in James 5:15?

10. What should an elder who has the gift to heal do in order to magnify this gift?

11. Should we seek out those who have this gift of healing rather than our fathers or home teachers?

12. Some suggest our spirits run our bodies; therefore, it is our spirit that heals our body perhaps in conjunction with the spirits of those giving blessings. Your opinion?

13. To what extent can Satan have control over our bodies and cause illness?

14. Many people outside our church have been healed. How can this be?

15. How important are the following: faith of the individual; faith of the person giving the blessing; priesthood authority; and God's will?

16. Should we give a blessing or ask for one if our lives are not right?

17. How do we know what to say in a blessing?

18. Is it really necessary to suffer all the physical pain in this life that many do?

19. What significance does placing a name on the temple altar have in healing the sick?

20. How can we make ourselves more available to others to give more blessings than we do now?

This book attempts to answer most of these questions where scripture and prophets have given clear answers. A few questions provoke speculation which creates interesting discussion but no conclusions. The collective wisdom of experienced faithful members gives added insight into illness and blessings.

About the time the first draft of this book was typed the Lakewood Second Ward high priest quorum discussed the "Spiritual Effects of Priesthood Blessings." The next week the young married Sunday School class also allowed me to ask these questions. I wanted to make sure my original perception about the need to give and receive more priesthood blessings in most LDS families was still valid. (It was!)

The comment was made, in class, that if we talked about blessings more frequently at church more members would ask for them and more fathers would encourage blessings in their homes. When directed by the spirit, elders would more frequently say something like, "If you desire a blessing before school starts please don't hesitate to ask" or "I'm prepared to give you a blessing if and when you want one."

Why Blessings Are Not Given

The brethren in the Sunday School class all agreed they should give more priesthood blessings and they gave the following reasons why they hesitate: "Do not feel worthy enough"; "Lack of faith in my ability"; "Worried about the outcome"; and "Not sure of procedure or what to say."

The sisters hesitated to ask or encourage their children to ask for a blessing because: "Father was usually uptight"; "Not sure of father's response"; "I got better before I got up courage to ask"; "The right moment or setting in which to ask never came"; "Husband doesn't like to give blessings."

One sister told me after class, "My husband once gave me a blessing and I got sicker."

A young elder told the class he used to hesitate to give blessings but since he has had several experiences with administration he now encourages his family and home teaching families to ask for blessings. He said, "I like the feeling I get during and after using my priesthood." With held-back emotion, a young couple expressed their wish that more time would be given to learning all aspects about blessings because they wanted more priesthood use in their home.

Teaching About Blessings

For several months after the emphasis for stakes and wards to become "tithing worthy" in 1983 had been made, the members of the Lakewood Second Ward were reminded in most meetings to pay a full tithe. I thought to myself, If only a portion of the time had been spent on talking about the father's patriarchal role in giving his family blessings, the impact for good on families would be significant. Of course this is true when we concentrate on any principle of the gospel. Priesthood blessings are only one of dozens of church benefits. Unfortunately, laying on of hands is overlooked or used infrequently in many Latter-day Saint homes.

Talking about blessings within the family is a good way to insure future requests for use of a father/patriarch's priesthood authority. During family home evening there should be teaching about gospel principles, including tithing and healing. At tithing settlement time I enjoy telling the following true story.

Having an audit by the Internal Revenue Service is very intimidating even if you believe you have the proof of all deductions. My audit was for income tax averaging, medical expenses, and church-related contributions. Why was I so nervous as I sat down with my pile of paper in front of the auditor's messy desk?

In a resigned voice the young anxious auditor said, "All right, Mr. Ward, let's get underway." It sounded like we would be there all day. As I took the thick rubber band off the papers, it shot out of my hand and struck the auditor's whiskered cheek. As he winced in pain I put up my hands in mock horror. He did not smile. What a way to begin an audit.

He found the tax averaging to be okay and he concluded that when you have lots of children, you have lots of medical bills. I was apprehensive as he studiously looked through the church contributions. I remembered my father, Karl Ward, telling me about an audit where he was challenged about all the deductible donations he had made to Virginia Ward. It also complicated matters for him since he was the bishop who signed the receipts for the old North Long Beach "Virginia Ward." I was bishop of the Lakewood

Second Ward and had signed, along with the financial clerk, my donation receipts.

Explaining to the auditor my obligation and desire to pay tithing, fast offering, building, budget and welfare was easy compared to what followed. I had taken $400 in deductions for mileage as bishop, for use of our home for seminary, firesides, activities and for some miscellaneous minor expenses—all legitimately deductible in a minister's capacity. Since I had no proof of these expenditures, he asked, "What does a bishop do?" Since he appeared to have time I detailed my duties.

He indicated that—based on a minister's average expenditures—I could have over a thousand dollars in deductions. Then he asked me why I had not listed the renumerations for my "ministerial services." I told him that all of the church leadership in The Church of Jesus Christ of Latter-day Saints at the local level were unpaid. He paused, frowned, and said, "You mean to say you have to pay all this money into the church to be eligible to do all the unpaid service you described a bishop does?" My big smile answered his question and bore testimony of a "peculiar people." He said, "You must really believe in what you are doing!"

This story helps my children feel good about paying their tithes and offerings. We should also teach our children about priesthood blessings. Stories about laying on of hands will impress upon young minds a father's faith and his desire to bless them.

I learned a valuable lesson from my son during a fast and testimony meeting when I sat back to enjoy the meeting like most of those present. During the meeting Karl said, "Dad, don't you have a testimony?" Incredible! I travel and bear my testimony in different stakes nearly every Sunday. Since I do share my testimony so often, the three or four times a year I bear testimony in my own ward may be depriving others of the opportunity. My son, however, had suddenly become aware of the meaning of testimony and he needed to hear mine. Guess who was the first one up the following fast Sunday? Our children need a constant reminder of our testimony and of our availability to give them blessings.

If we can suggest that a person pay tithing surely we can suggest that a person, when prompted by the spirit, ask for a blessing. A father/patriarch will look for spiritual experiences to relate to his family; to teach them "correct principles" so they will ask for his blessings before and after they learn to "govern themselves."

Becoming Knowledgeable About Blessings

If we are held up to be knowledgeable about, or a good example of, a certain subject we will be sought after to perform or give advice on that subject.

On one occasion, my wife and I were on vacation in Acapulco, Mexico, with other Zenith television dealers. We were talking to friends during the cocktail hour before dinner in the large conference room of a magnificent new nine-story hotel. Our friends, as usual, kept us supplied with soft drinks and orange juice as they consumed large amounts of liquor.

Suddenly the room began to sway. All those from California who were sober knew immediately that we were having an earthquake. Some dove under chairs since there were no tables. Sondra and I moved quickly to a corner wall. The earthquake rumbled with a shaking motion followed by sharp jerks. The large hand-carved doors leading into the room collapsed. The portable bar tipped over. Acoustical tiles and masonry fell from above. We were on the second floor so that when the wall we were crushed against moved and cracked open the corner pillar-support was exposed. We heard muttered prayers from people who expected the building above us to collapse.

Abruptly, the shaking ceased. It was amusing to see the plaster-covered faces of those stuck under chairs, the gulping of drinks by waiters, and the voice of the maitre d' calling, "No problem, no problem! Dinner will be served later—I think!"

The earthquake was the most severe in recent history with a magnitude of 6.6 on the Richter scale. Acapulco was the epicenter. As we sat outside that night during the continuous aftershocks, alert for a possible tidal wave, my wife and I were surrounded by vacationing easterners. We were sought out because we had a basic knowledge of earthquakes. Our reassuring words calmed nearly everyone, but one nervous lady said after two hours of earthquake talk, "I'm catching the first plane out of here—I don't care where it goes!" Our "Zenith" group gathered together and after the staggering intoxicated mariachi band was quieted, I was asked to offer a prayer for those assembled.

Sondra and I spent considerable time that moonlit night talking to others and to each other. As we walked slowly along the cracked cement paths we were grateful for our lives, our families, and for the plan of salvation. It was not the knowledge of fickle earthquakes that kept us calm. It was our knowledge of the gospel.

If a father is viewed as having a knowledge of blessings, he will be sought after to give blessings. If a father has a testimony of the gospel and experience in giving blessings, he will be asked to give them more often.

Being Accessible and Timely

If we want to be asked for help, we must be accessible and available as my sister, Susan, and my fiancee, Sondra, learned one day while they were in the Hotel Utah. They decided to visit the Prophet. A hotel maid pointed out President David O. McKay's room. Timidly they knocked on the prophet's door. To their surprise he opened it. They were too surprised to say anything until he invited them in. He apologized because Sister McKay could not greet them. She was sick in bed. He inquired about their families and schooling. When President David O. McKay learned about Sondra's engagement to "an older man of twenty-eight" he told her he had married at the age of twenty-nine and had been happily married for sixty-one years.

When the girls stood up to leave the Prophet, he shook their hands with both of his and, looking them directly in the eyes, thanked them for dropping by and he wished them the best in their future lives. Can we be that accessible, especially to persons who are in need of our blessing?

Opportunities to give blessings are lost if we are not available or if our timing is poor. Sometimes a person's desire for a blessing subsides rapidly. Perhaps when we attempt to follow perfect procedure we can miss a chance to give a priesthood blessing.

I could have easily missed blessing my son when he had a waterskiing accident. Perfect procedure was not followed yet the blessing was valid.

The incident happened at Lake Arrowhead. Because of recent intense development, the lake may be placid in the early morning with mirrored images of forest and sky but by noon, on weekends, the mountains reverberate with a deafening roar of super-charged boats pulling skiers faster than is safe. The once-quiet cove in front of our dock is a colorful circus of speed boats, rafts, sailboats, and outboards trying to avoid fallen skiers. The frantic waving of red flags by crewers for their downed skiers alert those manipulating boats among this zoo. We follow a rule based on sad experience that on summer Saturdays only exceptional skiers will face the misguided swells and waves.

Anticipating, on the morrow, a slow Sabbath my older children decided to challenge the cove. This was Joey's first summer to legally drive our 19-foot Century inboard ski boat. He was more than cautious which brought exasperated commands from the end of the ski rope where his seventeen-year-old brother, Michael, constantly sought more speed, a better route, or a bigger wake. While he was swinging into the cove for another pass in front of our dock Michael attempted a sharp cut. He hit a cross wave and fell hard. He flew out of his single ski and bounced on the water like a skipping rock which abruptly stops and sinks.

This time, instead of just being winded for a moment, it was obvious to the attentive crewer, his sister Lesa, that something was terribly wrong. There was no attempt by Michael to put on the ski that had pursued his path. He was unbelievably motionless in the cold water with his orange and black ski jacket keeping him afloat.

Lesa jerked up the red flag and shouted to Joey, "Mike's hurt!" Joey made the turn back without cutting r.p.m.s. The boat shot up out of the water as it hit competing swells so that only the full-powered prop remained in the water. Joey headed directly for Michael, pulling back the throttle at the last moment which caused the boat to suddenly settle down into the water.

Michael was dazed but conscious as his brother and sister helped him around the still prop and into the boat. Blood covered Michael, his ski jacket, and the back of the boat. The composite ski had knifed through the water after the bouncing Michael. When he stopped the ski struck his left ear and the side of his head. Weakly, Michael said, "Get me to the dock, fast." Joey drove full speed past the "5 mph" buoys.

Joey began a slow climb up to the cabin with Michael, but when they got to the road Michael was too dizzy to continue so Joey ran ahead for help. His call from below the cabin, "Mike's hurt bad!" sent me racing and slipping on the pine needles straight down the mountainside.

Michael, beginning to pass out, had flagged down a car while he stood in the road with his blood-soaked shirt pressed to his head. The "Good Samaritan" brought Michael up the dirt road and helped place him in Sondra's car. He said, "Hey man, don't worry about the blood on my car seat, it will wash off."

Lovely, conscientious, eleven-year-old Lesa had remained at the dock with her younger sisters. Arriving there out-of-breath I guessed I had somehow missed Michael in my shortcut rush down the hill. The girls and I hurried up to the road where Sondra met us with semi-conscious Michael in the back seat of her car. Sondra said, "Do you want a blessing, Mike?" He nodded, yes.

I could have blessed him there, but since the cabin and consecrated oil were only a steep block away I said to Sondra, "Drive us up to the cabin." When we got there Sondra ran inside to get the oil as I examined the gaping wound in Michael's head. Then, with a loving mother holding her son's hand in the back seat of the car, I anointed and sealed. The blessing promised, by the authority of the priesthood, that Michael's lacerated ear and damaged head would be made completely well and whole quickly with no problems or scars.

He was taken to the Mountain Hospital Emergency and then to a plastic surgeon in Riverside. The next day Michael sat against the wall at church so no one could see his stitched, grotesque-looking ear.

Two weeks later Michael received a father's blessing before he left to attend BYU. I noticed then that his ear and head were almost healed. The next week he commented, after I ordained him an elder, that there was hardly any physical sign that he had been in an accident.

If we had waited for a hurting Michael to ask for a blessing, tried to find another elder, waited for me to change into a suit, or taken time to fast and pray, the opportunity and immediate necessity to bless my son might have passed. Another wise comment from the Young Married's Sunday School class: "Better to be timely than correct."

When is it time to ask for a blessing? When is a person "sick enough" to be blessed? There was not a simple answer to that question for me until I recently stubbed my toes.

One lazy Sunday afternoon, cute seven-year-old Lindsay came to my bedroom door and with a sly smile said, "Daddy, dinner is ready. I'm going to beat you!" She assumed the "on your mark" position. As is the custom, I slowly got off the bed and strolled toward her until she took off with me charging close on her heels. This time I slipped and smashed my right foot into the doorjamb. I crumbled into a moaning heap. The family came running from the kitchen and stared down at my contorted, pained body. Sondra said, "What can I do?" Lindsay said, "I won!" I said, "Let me be; go eat!" I could hear nine-year-old, articulate Amy praying, "Bless the food before us, bless Michael at the 'Y', bless Karl on his mission, and bless Daddy on the floor."

Situated in bed with an ice pack on my four swollen toes, I began preparing for a fireside talk. Jim Wright came to visit. He asked, "Would you like a blessing?" I responded, "For stubbed toes?" We laughed, but if there had been another Melchizedek Priesthood holder present I probably would have said "Yes." Was I hurting enough to delay my friend's departure and disturb my home teacher? Besides, the pain was subsiding so, rather than inconvenience anyone, I declined the offer. Later, when I got off the bed, the excruciating pain shot through my foot and up my leg. I thought, "I'll never make it. Who can I get to give tonight's fireside talk?" Then I realized I needed a blessing!

There wasn't time to call our home teacher to bless my foot, so with my throbbing right foot in the passenger's seat and my left foot operating the accelerator and brake I arrived at the Cerritos Stake Center. I asked the Young Adult leader to arrange a blessing for me. A young elder haltingly performed his first anointing and the Young Adult leader blessed me to be able to "give my talk and go to work."

During the successful fireside talk my good leg went to sleep, so to keep from falling I hung onto the pulpit. One week later, X-rays showed two of my stubbed toes were actually broken. The doctor said "Don't jog for three to six months," which caused me more distress than the pain. With this knowledge I sought another blessing from my home teacher who promised "fast healing." Two weeks later I was cautiously jogging.

Since then, if injury or sickness restricts me from serving my God, my family, or my customers, I will, after prayerful confirmation, request a blessing.

Gift to Heal

During a high priest quorum meeting we were discussing whether we should look to the father or home teacher before seeking out someone with the "gift to heal." The consensus was that we should ask those closest to us to be voice during the sealing. During the lively exchange of ideas two members of the quorum were impressed to reveal to the rest that, according to their patriarchal blessings, they possessed the "gift to heal." Both said they felt that they should have done more with this gift and both men wondered how they might have avoided hiding their "talent in the earth" (Matt. 25:25). They wanted to know how they might magnify their gift and use it more frequently in the future.

Seven steps were suggested by quorum members: (1) learn all you can about priesthood blessings; (2) be worthy; (3) talk about your gift or blessings with your family; (4) take the initiative with younger children in giving blessings; (5) suggest to home teaching and extended families your desire to give them blessings when they need one; (6) let the quorum leader and bishop know you may be available for last-minute requests for blessings; and (7) pray to the Lord that you might be an instrument in His hands to bless His children.

I believe all Melchizedek Priesthood bearers who follow these basic suggestions will be asked to bless their families and others more often.

IV

Preparing to Give Blessings

We must be well prepared to give priesthood blessings so that we can give them correctly.

Follow Correct Procedure

The apostle James said, "Is any sick among you? Let him call for the elders of the church; and let them pray over him, anointing him with oil in the name of the Lord: And the prayer of faith shall save the sick, and the Lord shall raise him up." (James 5:14-15.) More detail in giving a healing blessing is found in John A. Widtsoe's book, *Priesthood and Church Government in The Church of Jesus Christ of Latter-day Saints* (1950, pp. 355-357).

> Administration should be made at the request of the sufferer or of someone vitally concerned, so that it may be done in answer to faith. One of the elders called in should pour oil on the crown of the head and anoint the sick person and while anointing, pray to the Father in the name of Jesus Christ for the restoration of the health of the sick brother or sister, but he should not seal the anointing. Oil for this anointing should be pure olive oil which has been consecrated for that purpose. Giving consecrated oil internally is not a part of the administration and should not be done.
>
> Two or more elders shall lay their hands on the head of the sick person, after he or she has been anointed, and one of the elders shall be the voice in the sealing of the anointing. After sealing the anointing, the one speaking may add such blessings upon the head of the sick person as the Spirit of the Lord may dictate, doing all in the name of Jesus Christ, and by virtue of the Holy Priesthood. It is permissible, if the Spirit of the Lord should indicate that it should be done, for the brethren to kneel in prayer before the administration but this is not an essential part of the ordinance of administering to the sick.

Instructions on the correct procedure for doing priesthood ordinances are discussed in quorum meetings. Those not holding the priesthood also participate in blessings by being present and combining their faith with the faith of those participating. Sondra usually holds our sick child as my son anoints and I seal the anointing. When I have been administered to by the elders, I have felt Sondra's faith by her presence.

Proper procedure can vary depending on the circumstances. Our Regional Representative, Elder Lloyd M. Rasmussen, told the following experience at stake conference:

Elder Spencer W. Kimball, then President of the Council of the Twelve, arrived in Brother Rasmussen's stake ill from a recent throat operation. He was there to reorganize the stake. After a full day and night of interviews and meetings, the tired Apostle went to President Rasmussen's home to stay the night. He asked that a comfortable chair be put in his room since he had difficulty sleeping lying down. As Brother Rasmussen walked past his door later, a whispered voice asked him to "Please come in." Elder Kimball was having difficulty trying to sleep. He said, "Would you please give me a blessing?" A complicated procedure could have transpired: such as calling for help late at night for another elder to anoint, etc. President Rasmussen simply asked the future president of the Church if he wanted an anointing or special blessing. At the mention of the latter, Elder Kimball said that would be fine. Tall President Rasmussen knelt beside the humble Apostle and placed his hands on the head of his special guest. Afterwards, Elder Kimball thanked him and showed him the hole in his throat and the chest scar from his recent heart surgery. It was an intimate moment shared by *two* great men. To have another elder present was not necessary on this occasion.

Instructions state that generally two or more elders lay their hands on the head of the sick person. "Generally" means there are exceptions to the "two or more" rule. Did I need oil and another elder to give Joey a blessing on the lonely sand dune? When your child wakes up at 3:00 a.m. with a fever do you overlook the blessing because you do not wish to disturb your home teacher? Melchizedek Priesthood bearers possess the authority to anoint and seal. When you are alone you can do both. It would be more correct to involve the home teacher or another Melchizedek Priesthood bearer, if one is available.

Sometimes exact procedures might not be followed because the "ox-is-in-the-mire." As the high councilman responsible for the Long Beach East College Branch elders quorum, I was in attendance at their sacrament meeting. After the meeting I was to conduct the ordination of an elder. The phone in the hallway interrupted the service by ringing several times before someone answered it. A note was sent to me to come to the phone. My wife said, "The police just called to say a car drove through the windows of the store. I called your brother, Bob, and he's going down." I said, "I'll go down after the ordination here." Sitting back in my seat, unable to concentrate on the service, I thought *How can you sit here and let your brother handle the obvious mess at the store?* Fortunately there was another high councilman present. I sent him a note asking that he take care of my assignment. When he nodded approval, I left.

A drunken driver had smashed his car through two windows into the displayed furniture. Glass was everywhere but so were brethren wearing white shirts and ties helping my brothers clean and board up the display windows. I recognized a bishop, a counselor, an elders quorum president and others. They had heard about the accident and had left their Sabbath meetings, too. Imagine the gratitude that welled up within me as I drove home thinking about the men who followed the "spirit of the law" rather than the "letter of the law." Always follow the spirit when giving blessings.

We assume those holding the Melchizedek Priesthood know how to give blessings, yet they need to learn about basic procedure before they perform that first ordinance. As an example, when a recent Cambodian convert to the Church came to visit our home with her extended family of refugee children, they faced the unfamiliar. After rounding up bathing suits for the ten shy Cambodian children I unlocked the pool's gate. Two minutes later I had to jump in and save a teenager and two children from drowning. They had never been in a swimming pool and did not know that one end was deeper than the other. Elders should not have to fear the unfamiliar "pool" of giving blessings. They should learn to "swim" with proper training and experience.

One of my first experiences in administering to the sick could have been my last. My missionary companion and I were awakened from a deep sleep at 4:00 a.m. to heal a dying old man. We became wide awake riding our bikes in the chilling cold across the moors near Barnsley, England. We were ushered into a small stuffy room by several sobbing relatives. Their instructions to us were simple: "Heal him." My first impulse was to say to the sick man, "Rise, take up thy bed and walk" (John 5:1-16). But it was obvious even to me, who had never seen a dead person, that the spirit had departed from this man some time ago. My companion and I looked at each other, stood erect, anointed with oil, placed our hands on the cold, hard, bald head of the dead man and blessed his eternal progression and his grieving family.

Even without much training, the spirit will guide the humble efforts of novice, worthy priesthood bearers.

Listen to the Spirit

Important things to do when giving any kind of a blessing are to close your eyes, shut out the distracting surroundings and, after saying the basic opening prayer words, listen—listen for the promptings of the spirit. If you are overly aware of the grieving family, the nurses, the medical odors, the feverish patient, or the non-member onlookers you may become distracted. It was President Zimmerman who taught me to close my eyes, say the proper phrases, then pause—listen—catch my breath, and then continue.

Be positive. Remember to bless those who treat and care for the patient. Sometimes family members, too, need a special blessing to help them with their emotional suffering. The spirit of the Lord must guide your thoughts and words. We should not command a person to be made well if it is not God's will. When we have no assurance of healing, our blessing becomes a prayer for God's help that "His will be done" rather than a promise that the person be made well.

A father, who was not a member of the Church, asked me to do what I could for his hospitalized son. The college student was in a coma caused by an overdose of drugs. I sat there in the small, dim room alone with the tan, muscular young man. He appeared to sleep except for his deep, labored, wheezy breathing. The home teacher was on his way to assist with the blessing. The mother was a member of the Church and as she and her husband waited in the hospital visitor's room, I prayed for guidance. I wanted this young man with such great potential to live! This could be a turning point in his family—a time to recognize the priesthood, for the husband to join the Church, and to live the gospel. The more I prayed the more I realized that my "cause was just," but the spirit was leading me to another conclusion. The home teacher and I both were aware that our prayer was a supplication for divine help for the youth and his family rather than a command to be healed. We were not surprised by his death that evening.

In any blessing or "mighty prayer" the spirit must be present to direct the prayer then give the answer. Learn to recognize the answer. Be careful, however, not to confuse an emotional experience with a spiritual one.

At BYU, I was introduced to the music room by my freshman friend, Craig Carpenter. During our lunch hours we would put on headsets and direct the famous orchestras of the world. Our flailing arms in this silent room were out of place to the infrequent observer. The first time I put on the headset and listened to Brahms' First Symphony in C-minor I thought I was having a religious experience, but what I really felt was emotion from hearing a spectacular performance. Entering the cathedral in York, England, with its high arches formed by flying buttresses, and hearing rich bass sounds coming from the massive antique organ gave me another emotional experience. Emotional and spiritual experiences can combine, but the Spirit must witness to your soul the answer to your prayers.

Dreams can also be an unreliable source of supposed revelation for some. My dreams seem to be caused by what I eat or by highly stressful days. Fortunately, we are not held accountable for what we dream. Even though I pay little attention to dreams, I have built a secure fence around our pool and made sure the children learn to swim while they are infants. This preparation is a result of several child-drowning dreams I have had. Some people's dreams may have significance; if so, there should be a spiritual confirmation and interpretation. The only dream I can remember that may have had significance occurred while I was living in the basement of the Val Hyric house in Provo, Utah. I was a senior at BYU, in 1956, when they separated the two large campus branches into a stake and wards. I was disappointed when it appeared to me that all the positions were filled in my new ward. Here I was preparing for a mission with no opportunity to serve.

On a Wednesday night I knelt on the damp floor of my room pleading for an opportunity to serve. That night I dreamed that my friend, Drew Crowley, who was then serving a mission in France, sat on my bed and said not to worry. "You will serve the Lord." I awoke and had a warm, comforting, long-lasting, happy sensation.

A week later, I was called to teach the elders quorum. As I began my first lesson, I expressed my apprehension of teaching so many returned missionaries. Afterwards, the elders quorum president thanked me and said, "Brother John will do fine. The Lord called him. A week ago Wednesday I was going through the card file of quorum members trying to choose a teacher. I stopped, picked up a discarded card and read 'John Ward.' I had never heard of him. It was, however, plainly revealed to me that he should teach this quorum." (That dream was so real that a few years later I asked Drew if he had ever left his mission and visited me. He laughed!)

A good example of looking for an answer to prayer—and recognizing the answer when it comes—took place when the Church switched from the M-Men and Gleaners to the Young Adult program. The program was designed to be "flexible" in order to meet the needs of the Young Adults. The new stake Young Adult council had wrestled all summer with the stake format of classes and activities. What format would involve the most Young Adults and still maintain quality?

On the final Sunday, before we needed to print our calendar and begin our program, we all met after fasting. We experienced the presence of the Lord's spirit in that meeting. Tears were shed as we said "Yes" to one good idea after another. There was, however, no final consensus on how to "package" the ideas. Sitting up front at the fireside that evening as the high council advisor, trying to look dignified, I prayed with my eyes open. Those hundred souls in front of me—and those not present—had so many needs.

Kneeling that night before retiring I poured out my heart. I reminded the Lord of the great effort put forth in establishing the best possible program. Lying in bed thinking about the council meeting I suddenly had the answer. I shouted for joy. "That's it!" I turned on the light, kissed my wife, told her to go back to sleep, and began to write furiously, afraid I might lose the light burning within my heart and mind. I made reams of notes incorporating every reasonable suggestion from the day's meeting and past council meetings.

When I finished early in the morning, I knelt and gave thanks, lay back, and basked in the peace present in that bedroom.

President Marion G. Romney described several years ago what I had just glimpsed: "After praying and on many occasions fasting for a day each week over long periods of time, I have had answers revealed to my mind in finished sentences. I have heard the voice of God in my mind and I know his words." (*Look to God and Live*, pp. 44-45.) Our inspired Young Adult format was unchanged for many years. Hundreds were friendshipped and activated.

An answer to prayer will usually be clear and precise with a feeling that the Holy Ghost is with you. There is an accompanying peace and joy. An important procedure in giving a blessing is to listen. An important procedure in receiving inspiration is to listen. Listen to know what to pray for and listen to receive the answer.

Dress Appropriately

A certain amount of preparation right after being asked to give a blessing is needed for an administration to be "effectual." One Saturday morning as I was trying to thin out the suffocating flowers planted by tossing seeds at random a few weeks earlier, Sondra came outside to tell me that Sister Anderson had called and asked that I give her husband a blessing. I washed my muddy hands and called back to ask if it was an emergency. "No, he has been ill for some time and is getting worse," she replied. I told her that I would be there in 45 minutes.

There was now time to shave, shower, put on a suit and pray. Walking to the car I stopped to look at the blooming array of flowers. Take time to smell the roses. There is no need to rush to give most blessings. Take time to prepare yourself. However, there are exceptions.

While I was playing tennis on the Long Beach City College courts my wife came running up to the high fence. She thrust the bottle of consecrated oil in my hand as she caught her breath and said, "Hurry, honey, Sister Huntsman had a car accident and is dying at the Los Altos Hospital." I ran for my car leaving my wife to explain to my atheist partner my hurried departure.

I was running down the long shiny corridor of the hospital in my tennis outfit looking for Velma Huntsman. A burly nurse suddenly spread her arms, blocking the way. In a gruff voice, she asked, "Hey, where do you think you're going?" Trying to sound as dignified as possible, I said, "I'm a minister!" She interrupted my explanation with "You're kidding!" If I had been dressed properly it would have taken less time to persuade her to give me Sister Huntsman's location.

When I give a blessing I feel more comfortable in my "church uniform," which consists of a dark suit, white shirt, and conservative tie. When I am dressed in a basketball uniform, I feel like floating from the top of the key to the basket. Wearing my camouflaged army combat fatigues, I am ready for a fight. When we had formal dances at "Friday Night in Long Beach" with everyone in formal dress, there was seldom a problem but when we had western or grubby-dress dances, we always had behavior problems. You act like you dress because you feel like you look. To give a formal priesthood blessing, when possible, look the part.

There are other reasons to dress appropriately. Once a member of our ward came to the bishop's office to complain about one of the priests at the sacrament table. This sixteen-year-old priest had come a long way in his desire to be active in the Church again. Several of the youth and adults were doing all they could to help this young man with his problems. I agreed with the concerned ward member that the young man's long, flowing, blond hair might detract from the sacredness of the sacrament. He was worthy to be a priest; therefore, worthy to bless the sacrament. Yes, I had counseled him on being well-groomed—and he was. According to the girls he was the "best looking of the bunch."

As the member who had complained realized I would not "ban" the young priest from the sacrament table he became a little upset. I told the brother that the priest looked a lot like the person in the picture on the wall behind him. He turned his head to look and as he turned back toward me he had a big smile on his face. He had noticed the long hair of Jesus Christ.

I may have failed this youth. I was afraid of being too stern for fear of losing him. Because of his "hippie" appearance at school he attracted youth of a similar look with much lower standards. He succumbed to the daily temptations offered him by his surfing "buddies." Only after his family moved and he cut his hair did he repent and begin his gospel progression again. When we look the part we act the part.

At home I have given blessings in my pajamas and in my grubby clothes. Some men dress in a suit to give blessings to their families. Are these extremes? Whatever is needed to help you give the best blessing possible to your sick child is what you should do.

Bless When Ready

One night Sondra tried to wake me out of a deep sleep. She was sick and wanted to be healed. I mumbled something about "Give me a chance, will you!" She was upset and said, "Never mind." After discussing this the next day, she and the children now occasionally say, "When you are ready, will you please give me a blessing?" My response is always "Yes" and before the day is over I have had time to prepare myself to call down the blessings of heaven upon their heads. This preparation time allows me to try to repent of any wrong doing. Repentance in this sense is usually to stop doing what is wrong and start doing what is right.

I once said to a Young Adult leader, "Have you had a blessing for that bad cold?" So many young people believe having a cold is not reason enough to get a priesthood blessing yet a persistent cold can drag a person down physically and spiritually. Her response was sad: "My father does not give blessings."

I told her that men in general have a difficult time giving blessings. It is hard to change hats from working in the materialistic world to dealing with things of the Spirit. The transition takes time. I suggested that she ask her father for a blessing when he felt ready. The following week she reported to me with tears of joy that she had received a "marvelous blessing" the day after asking. She said, "It was a choice experience for me and the whole family. We all cried." She was better, too! Rather than deny children a blessing (they may not ask again) tell them a preparation time is necessary in order for you to feel more worthy. This will bind them close to their father/patriarch.

Apostle Ezra Taft Benson tells a similar story:

> I had a young man come to my office the other day asking for a blessing. He was eighteen years-of-age, and he had problems. There were no serious moral problems but he was all mixed up in his thinking and worried, and he asked if he could have a blessing. I said to him, "Have you ever asked your father to give you a blessing? Your father is a member of the Church, I assume?" He said, "Yes, he is an elder, a rather inactive elder." When I said, "You love your father?" he replied "Yes, Brother Benson, he is a good man. I love him." He then said, "He doesn't attend to his priesthood duties as he should. He doesn't go to Church regularly. I don't know that he is a tithe payer, but he is a good man." I said, "How would you like to go to him, go back to your home and talk to him at the opportune time, and ask him if he would be willing to give you a father's blessing?" "Oh," he said, "I think that would frighten him." I then said, "Are you willing to try it? I will be praying for you." He said, "All right, on that basis, I will."
>
> Three or four days later he came back. He said, "Brother Benson, that's the greatest thing that has happened in our family." And he could hardly control his feelings as he told me what had happened. He said, "When the opportunity was right, I mentioned it to father, and mother was there and two or three of the younger children, and he said, 'Son, do you really want me to do that?' I said 'Yes, Dad, I would like you to.' " And he said, "Brother Benson, he gave me one of the most beautiful blessings you could ever ask for." He said, "Mother sat there crying all during the blessing. When we got through there was a bond of appreciation and gratitude and love which we have never had in our home." ("My Errand From The Lord" A Personal Study Guide, The Church of Jesus Christ of Latter-day Saints. 1976-1977.)

Wife Sustains Husband

In my church experience it seems that women are consistently more spiritual than men. They progress through life without the sharp peaks and valleys of spirituality most men regularly experience. Maybe this is why more women will gain exaltation than men will. Most sisters appear to have the staying power to sustain themselves and their husbands through spiritual lows. Few men become "spiritual giants" without a "spiritual giant" for a wife, yet I have met many women who have achieved great spirituality without a sustaining husband. The sisters seem to do better in their role as mothers than men do in their role as fathers. The sisters long for worthy men who will use their priesthood to bless their lives. Priesthood holders have the potential to reach great heights and they do, especially during a blessing. Men in general have difficulty in sustaining the "spiritual high." Sometimes I am exhausted at the conclusion of a priesthood blessing. The lingering spirituality is easily destroyed by turning on the T.V. or going back to work. When emergencies occur, most priesthood bearers do instantly react properly as the Lord sustains them. He will sustain them on a daily basis, too, if they let Him.

The Lord has cautioned men ". . . that the powers of heaven cannot be controlled nor handled only upon the principles of righteousness . . . in any degree of unrighteousness . . . the Spirit of the Lord is grieved; and when it is withdrawn, Amen to the priesthood or authority of that man. . . . We have learned by sad experience that it is the nature and disposition of almost all men, as soon as they get a little authority, as they suppose, they will immediately begin to exercise unrighteous dominion." (D&C 121:34-46.) The sisters also need to understand all the verses in this section so that they may help their eternal mates. A greater understanding of "righteous dominion" might have lessened the heartache of our first marital argument.

We had just moved into our first home two blocks from the Long Beach Fourth Ward. Sondra said, "Let's put the baby in the stroller and walk to church. Then we can leave the stroller in the foyer." I said "No, we shouldn't put the stroller in the foyer." This simple discussion went back and forth and finally I made the biggest mistake of our fledgling marriage. I said, "I'm the head of this family. Leave the stroller home!" Fortunately, my unrighteous command was over something trivial. I learned quickly the meaning of being equals; of using my priesthood ". . . by persuasion, by long-suffering, by gentleness and meekness, and by love unfeigned . . ." (D&C 121:41). It is nearly impossible to function as a true father/patriarch without a happy, sustaining wife.

Become Worthy

Not being worthy to give a blessing can result in an unsettling situation. How do you refuse a request: "I'm sorry, I'm not living right; better ask someone else"? My wife and I, on a wedding anniversary, mistakingly saw an "R" rated movie. The foul language did not bother me (it did Sondra), for those years in the army have "seared my conscience." Only one brief scene upset me. The gross portrayal was branded in my brain. The next evening a high council meeting was held. I did not attend. Knowing I was without the spirit I felt unworthy. During the days it took me to erase the memory, I feared being asked to bless someone. I actually avoided a sick person I thought might ask me for a blessing.

President David O. McKay has described how one begins the process of feeling worthy to act in God's name:

What progress can there be for a man unconscious of his faults? Such a man has lost the fundamental element of growth, which is the realization that there is something bigger, better, and more desirable than the condition in which he now finds himself . . . The greatest of faults is to be conscious of none. ("The Necessity of Repentance," *Improvement Era*, Mar. 1959, p. 143.)

All priesthood bearers have faults. If they refused to perform priesthood duties until they felt totally worthy, few blessings would ever be given. Many brethren hesitate because they feel unworthy to receive inspiration and they fear that this might cause a blessing to be invalid. However, to ask a priesthood holder for a blessing causes him to consider his faults, pray for forgiveness, and become a better person. Sometimes, asking a priesthood bearer to give a blessing might be the catalyst that places him on the "straight and narrow road" to being active in the Church and a true father/patriarch.

My teen-age son, Michael, had an experience that dramatically shows the need to be worthy to receive inspiration from God. On a Memorial Day weekend vacation, four of my boys and I went to church in Lebec, California. We must have looked strange to the dirt-bike riders as we drove, in our white shirts and ties, past the golden, poppy-covered off-road vehicle area near our camp. And we must have looked equally strange to Lebec ward members as we drove up with our motor home towing a trailer loaded with dusty, red dirt bikes. But, even in the high desert, our family outings begin with prayer and include church attendance and Sabbath observance.

On Monday, fifteen-year-old Michael expressed his gratitude for prayer and for having gone to church. He experienced the protective whispering of the Holy Ghost. Michael gave a talk at a stake youth fireside about what happened just before we broke camp:

> I was riding motorcycles with my dad exploring a new area. We really hadn't ridden very long when Dad hit a yucca plant and got a flat tire. He stayed back at camp while I went riding by myself. Nobody was around as I climbed a steep hill at full speed. Usually, I would have kept the throttle wide open to see what kind of jump I could get coming off the other side. This time was different. I received an experience that I will never forget. As I approached the top of the hill I had the strongest impression to stop! I really didn't want to stop, but my foot and hand moved to the brakes without any conscious thought from me. I came to an abrupt stop at the top of the hill. As I looked down at the incredibly steep, rocky hill and the cut barbed-wire fence, my stomach jumped. I started shaking and my eyes were watering. I had stopped less than six feet from the edge of a 100-foot drop off.
>
> I looked back at the long skid in the dirt and thought to myself: Even if I could have somehow survived the long fall, it would have been a long time before anyone found me. Nobody would have seen me go and my dad was over a mile away.
>
> I was glad to be alive. I thanked the Lord as I slowly rode back to camp where I told my dad what had happened. We both knew that I had received this warning to stop from the Holy Ghost."

Michael continued his story showing that he has learned, at a young age, the
necessity of being worthy to receive inspiration:

> A few weeks later I was ordained a priest, and I was glad to be one. I was
> worthy to receive the office and I was worthy to receive the protection that I
> did get while I was motorcycling. I often think what the circumstances would
> have been if I hadn't been worthy to receive the protection. What if, instead of
> a prayer before the trip, we'd had a six-pack of beer? What if I had gone out
> and done something wrong the week before and had not repented? Would I
> have stopped before the edge? I don't think so! So, what do I do now? Do I
> repent of all my sins every time I go motorcycle riding and then, when I get
> home, go and live-it-up with my friends until the next trip? No! I need to be
> worthy to receive help and guidance in everything I do every day; not just
> motorcycling!

This same wise thinking applies to giving an effectual blessing.

Avoid Appearance of Evil

Members will not ask you for blessings if you give the appearance of
being unworthy. On one occasion I was in danger of losing my credibility
with the Young Adults I advised. Across the street from our family store is a
Mexican restaurant. Sitting at my usual table, I began reading the newspaper
while I waited for the waitress to clear the table and take my order. Some
Young Adults from my stake came in to eat. I knew they had seen me but
they refused to catch my eye. Then the waitress cleaned my table and the
Young Adults all jumped up, came over, shook my hand and chatted.
Strange behavior, I thought: then I understood. When they came in, I was
munching on the leftover basket of chips next to the half-empty wine glass
and beer bottle.

It is important to "Abstain from all appearance of evil" (1 Thes. 5:22).
Who would ever ask for priesthood help from, or sustain, a person whom
they thought was unworthy?

If we just try to live Church standards those who are not members of
our church will help us to live them. When I attend one of our store's business association meetings, milk or 7-Up is always at my seating place. In
time, the swearing and smoking near me have ceased. I never asked for this.
And during a Senate Select Committee hearing on interest rates, I was asked
to present the Association's views. I asked "Why me?" My friend responded,
"The board decided you are the only one they would believe." Respect
follows those who are trying to live high standards.

Sondra and I were in Portugal once with a tour group. We spent all day
touring the beautiful, but hot, countryside. The only soft drinks available
to us were cokes, which we declined. By the time we were ushered into
dinner at the casino outside Lisbon we were "dying of thirst." Two long-
stemmed wine glasses were at each place setting. Bottles of red and white
wines adorned the long, Moorish tables. "Where are the water glasses?" I

asked Sondra. Hoping "agua" sounded like water in Portuguese I asked for some from the nearest waiter. He said, in broken English, "Vater for vashing hands?" Unable to communicate with me further, he left. Was the water bad? I sat looking at the wine another waiter had just poured in our glasses. As I contemplated my first strong drink, a sociable well-dressed lady across from us said, "You're Mormons, aren't you?" Her son was attending BYU and she had questions about the Church which we tried to answer. We spent a pleasant evening together and Sondra and I survived by eating all table decorations which consisted of grapes. Would the woman have talked about her son at BYU, or promised to look up the missionaries, if I had drunk that wine? I do not think so. If we are to bless the lives of people we must live exemplary Church standards.

I had difficulty gaining the respect of the youth of the Long Beach Second Ward. I was unable to bless their lives for awhile because of an unthinking, foolish incident.

Sondra and I were newly married and managing our apartments. Having been recently set apart as a counselor to Bishop Jay Spongberg, I was looking forward to working with the youth. On a moonless night I heard, from our apartment, noises down by the pool. The pool's submerged, bluish light reflected on the toilet paper floating in the water. The neighborhood kids had occasionally tossed trash barrels over the fence and into the pool.

Can you imagine what it's like to clean trash and garbage out of a pool? I flipped! The anger raged as I bounded down the stairs after the culprits hiding in the shadows. Words never used before, but placed in the recesses of my mind during basic training at Fort Ord, exploded from my mouth. There were many kids and I chased some of them for a block venting my anger verbally. I had stopped them before they could mess up the pool. Luckily, only a few pieces of toilet paper needed to be cleaned up.

On Sunday most of the adults greeted me warmly but the youth avoided me like the plague. Then a Laurel teacher explained to me that after MIA a group of youth went to our apartment complex to welcome us into the ward by toilet papering the place. My only comment as I turned crimson was "Oh, no!"

Sustain Priesthood Authority

To give effectual priesthood blessings it is important to accept church callings, and to sustain general and local authorities. When we accept any church position we put outselves in a position to serve others. We do things for others we might not normally do. In serving there is the promise of Jesus that, by losing ourselves, we find ourselves. (Matt. 10:39.)

We should not actively seek a Church calling by promoting ourselves or by campaigning. It is all right to desire a position but not when there is difficulty getting over the disappointment of not being chosen. "This is a true saying, If a man desire the office of a bishop, he desireth a good work." (1 Tim. 3:1.) The Lord has prepared members for their callings and because of "desire" many are not surprised when a particular calling comes.

I had the privilege of serving as bishop while President Raymond Linford served as president of the Long Beach East Stake. Early one morning, while he was playing basketball, President Linford called for a "time out" — and he died.

Several people suggested to me that I might be called to be in the new stake presidency. This was not to be, and on the morning of stake conference the disappointment came as I prayed for the Lord's help in continuing to be a good bishop and in supporting our new stake presidency. I raised my hand high in sustaining the new presidency called of God. The disappointment was gone that afternoon. Looking back, how could I have desired to miss the six years of joy I spent as Young Adult advisor and the fruitful years as counselor to the California Los Angeles mission president? The Lord knows where we are needed and what is best for us.

When we raise our hands to sustain anyone, we are stating our willingness to support them. I have never had a church leader I could not sustain. There have been differences of opinion in the early stages of decision making, but once those called by the Lord to lead have made the choice, I sustain wholeheartedly their decision. When I do so my family is blessed.

In the community you speak up within the system (politics) to bring about change. You have one vote. In church councils decisions are not usually put to a vote. There is no politicking. A consensus develops with discussion. The "Spirit bears witness" and the leader decides with unanimous support. It can be this way within families, too. As we learn to lead our families in this manner, as true father/patriarchs, we are better prepared to lead within the church and community. "For if a man know not how to rule his own house, how shall he take care of the Church of God?" (1 Tim. 3:5.) As we serve and sustain priesthood authority within the Church, we become better prepared to serve our families.

Speaking Up Within the Church

The head of this Church, Jesus Christ, speaks to the Church members collectively through his oracle, the prophet. The Lord speaks to us individually in answer to prayer. Our individual inspiration will not be in opposition, about church matters, to the divine guidance of leaders called to preside over us. The Prophet Joseph Smith said:

> I will inform you that it is contrary to the economy of God for any member of the Church, or any one, to receive instruction for those in authority, higher than themselves; therefore you will see the impropriety of giving heed to them;

but if any person have a vision or a visitation from a heavenly messenger, it must be for his own benefit and instruction. (*Teachings of the Prophet Joseph Smith*, p. 21.)

However, policy does get changed sometimes by someone "in the ranks" speaking up—not obnoxiously—but always in a reasonable forum. Most church leaders and parents want constructive criticism at the right time and place. This is how we improve.

After my first youth council meeting a teenage girl said to me, "Bishop, we never do anything we plan!" It took courage for her to say that. She wanted excellence in our ward's youth program. She wanted something better than mediocrity. In our next meeting we all resolved to do everything we planned. This caused us to plan very carefully. Since we had scheduled an overnight Christmas vacation snow trip, we went even though the highway patrol told us the roads were closed. They were closed and we had a fun, long drive up and back the same day. We were proud to have adhered to our policy. This one young girl caused us to have many more quality youth activities than we might normally have had. Since "The spirituality of a ward is commensurate with the activity of its youth" (David O. McKay), her courageous input helped the whole ward.

Speaking as a concerned church member is a privilege inherent in the Church. If, after prayer, a person feels good about a cause or dream, no matter how insignificant it may seem, they should make an appointment with their bishop to discuss it.

Represent Christ

In performing any priesthood duty it is important to remember that we represent Jesus Christ and act accordingly. Articles about my involvement with the School Board were in the local paper almost weekly for five years. Some of the time the article or editorial would state that I was a "Mormon." I would pray daily that my conduct would be representative of LDS beliefs. To the school's 7,000 employees, and much of the community, I represented the "Mormon Church." When making unpopular decisions I would think, What would Christ do? I never raised my voice and said, "Ye hypocrites" although it may have been appropriate a few times. My wife reminded me once, while I was tackling a momentous decision, that "Christ would probably not have been elected."

Ultimately, the editorials and articles became supportive as our schools improved. Once I talked to the paper's editor about why, out of twenty-six candidates for the Board and why, out of five Board members, my religion was the only one ever mentioned? "Mormons are not a curiosity any longer. The Church of Jesus Christ of Latter-day Saints is the second largest denomination in California," I explained. I asked him to use our proper name instead of "Mormon Church." The next editorial was favorable, and it referred to me as a "devout Mormon." When you represent your church as well as yourself it is easier to live the commandments and make good decisions.

I once gave a high council talk on "Being Proud to Be a Mormon." I always have been! "Mormon" is a nickname given to us by the mobs during the early Church days because of our belief in the *Book of Mormon*. The "big lie" being circulated by Satan today is that "Mormons" are not Christians, but a cult. As I reasoned to get Christmas carols, such as "Silent Night" and prayers at Vespers that mentioned Christ back in our schools, an administrator said to me, "I didn't know Mormons believed in Christ." While I was on a panel representing different religions, I asked the audience of high school students, "How many believe 'Mormons' are Christians?" The three raised hands belonged to "Mormons." I told the assembly, "That hurts, for we love our Savior, Jesus Christ."

I once called the Campus Crusade for Christ to rent their historic conference facility in San Bernardino for a bishop's seminar. The cheery young lady cleared the date and said "What was the name of your church again?" I gave her the name the second time and added, "We are commonly referred to as 'Mormons.' " There was a stillness, then obviously embarrassed, she politely said, "Oh, I am sorry, we only rent our facilities to Christians." I explained our correct full name and our belief in Christ. She said, "I'm sorry; your church is not on our list!" Not wanting to be a problem I thanked her and hung up.

We are not on a lot of people's list of those who are Christian. We are, perhaps, guilty of perpetuating myths about "Mormons" by not using our correct name. A statement on missionary work in 1982 sent to church leaders stated ". . . some may be misled by the too-frequent use of the term 'Mormon Church.' " We should use the name revealed to us in D&C 115:3-4. We need to do more of what the Nephites did: "We talk of Christ, we rejoice in Christ, we preach of Christ, we prophecy of Christ . . ." (2 Nephi 25:23-26). By becoming more Christ-centered, people will recognize the priesthood authority to act in Christ's name and request its use.

Relationship to God and Universe

A knowledge of Christ, God, and mankinds' eternal relationship to diety and the universe, will make our prayers and blessings more meaningful. For a short time I enjoyed a glimpse of what might be.

I gave my children a choice of places to go on a Thanksgiving holiday. They picked Death Valley because it sounded scarey. We drove into the desolate valley under a brilliant, silver-lined, orange sunset. The camps were full so we followed signs directing us and other motor homes off the road and into the bleak desert where we sank in the soft, red sand. The blowing sand blotted out the brilliant rising sun the next morning as fellow campers helped each other dig their way out to the highway. We briefly visited some scenic sites. The sand had shut down the generator that created voltage for the roof air conditioner. As the temperature rose to over 105 degrees, we drove up from Death Valley to the anticipated cool water at Owen's Lake. We were disappointed to find that the shimmering lake was a dry salt bed.

A sign pointed to Dirty Sock Springs and to us "spring" meant water. It was a hot mineral spring with an accompanying odor of rotten eggs. Joey and Bobby wanted to go swimming. After examining the thick blackish-green sludge covering the surface of the pond which appeared to be only algae, I said, "Why not?" Eventually everyone but Sondra and baby Lindsay were swimming. They were waving to us from the dirty motor home window. I was right over the hot bubbles with beautiful little Amy and Lesa holding on to me as we splashed the algae away. The boys were laughing as they attempted to walk on the slimy, slippery bottom. They actually invited the girls to play with them.

Alone, I heard my family's happy sounds as the sun left behind an orange blanket which covered the vastness of Mt. Whitney's majestic 14,495-foot elevation and Death Valley's 282 feet below sea level. I could see, in the distance, God's magnificent creations. Close by were multi-colored, rugged rock formations. How long had it taken God to create these wonders? I pondered. Remembering the millions of sand particles that covered the inside of our motor home and ruined the generator my thoughts turned to Moses 7:30: "And were it possible that man could number the particles of the earth, yea, millions of earths like this, it would not be a beginning to the number of thy creations; and thy curtains are stretched out still; and yet thou art there. . . ." Wow, I thought to myself. How many eons of eternity would it take for me to create a rock or this simplest form of life on my hand, a single-cell algae? Is it possible?

I got that warm feeling. Was it the hot bubbles, the spirit, or was it exhilaration from the heavenly beauty surrounding me that I felt? Moses 1:38-39 came to my remembrance: ". . . as one earth shall pass away, and the heavens thereof even so shall another come, and there is no end to my works, neither to my words. For behold, this is my work and my glory—to bring to pass the immortality and eternal life of man." I knew then that eternal life with God and Christ was a reality—a possible goal for my family.

How long would it take under God's and Christ's tutorship to create and to participate in the expanding universe? My finite mind had glimpsed eternity and could penetrate no further. The baby fell asleep and Sondra sat on the pond's bank near me; together "through all eternity" because we "have no end." At moments like this one feels the power to "bind in heaven and on earth." Those with priesthood authority can call down the power of heaven to bless peoples' lives. The feeling returns as we prepare and worthily pronounce a blessing with the Spirit within us. Our personal knowledge of God, the surety of life beyond the grave, and our burning testimony of the restoration of this Church by Jesus Christ prepares us to give blessings with confidence!

V

Results to Be Expected from Blessings

When a person is properly prepared to give a blessing and does it correctly, the recipient will be blessed. Sometimes the results of a prayer or blessing are immediately recognizable. More often, the results take time.

Immediate Results

After the Lakewood Second Ward's annual Christmas party, my eleven-year-old son, enjoyable Joey, said as he entered the house, "Quick, Dad, give me a blessing." As he ran for the bathroom, I ran for the consecrated oil. There was not time to call the home teacher. Joey was going to vomit as had most of the family due to the flu during the past week. With consecrated oil in hand I paused at the bathroom door. Joey was kneeling on the cold, hard, tiled floor talking to God. I did not interrupt because I had never heard a youth speak to God as "one man speaketh to another." You could feel the Spirit of the Lord in that small bathroom. Finally, interrupting a special moment, I said, "Joey, are you ready for a blessing?" He was, and as he sat on the toilet seat I anointed and then sealed the anointing and blessed him to be well. Afterwards he said, "I'm okay now." As he eased into his bed I offered to get him a trash can and towel in case of an emergency. (So much for my faith.) He said, "I'm better!" and went right to sleep. He was the only one in the family with the flu who did not throw up. He was probably healed before the blessing by his own sweet faith. He pleaded his case on a personal basis with God and was answered immediately.

On a Saturday I came down with the twenty-four-hour flu which was plaguing our family, and on Sunday I was supposed to conduct nine meetings and hold several important interviews. I was so sick it caused me to be late for the 6:30 a.m. bishopric meeting. I asked my counselors to give me a blessing to get me through the day. They pronounced me well and it was a rewarding Sunday filled with spiritual meetings and successful interviews. Coming home late Sunday night I was bone tired but happy. Monday morning I was again sick! The twenty-four-hour flu had been postponed—I had gotten "through the Sabbath day" as requested.

The immediate results of prayer, fasting, and a blessing benefited a fifteen-year-old girl. During MIA, a petite Mia Maid with head bowed mumbled, "Bishop, may I talk to you?" "Sure, come to my office." I said. This normally vivacious youth sat in a chair at the side of my desk with hands tightly clasped together unable to speak. I offered words of encouragement as she began to cry and handed her a tissue from the "year's supply" in the desk drawer. She sobbed that she had been "Too afraid to come." Her entire Mia Maid class was aware of her problem and they were fasting for her to have a successful interview with the bishop. She told me, "They talked me into coming." Gradually she related her indiscretions. She was deeply sorrowful and had been trying to repent for her first, brief flirtation with immorality. We talked about repentance. As she was leaving I was impressed to say, "Would you like a blessing to help you to repent?" My counselor assisted me in giving her a special blessing. She left knowing the Lord loved her and we knew she would be fine.

That night while praying for her I knew she had repented. The Lord bore witness to me that she was forgiven. The next morning I went to work and, during the hectic day, I forgot about the repentant Mia Maid. On Friday I got a letter from her thanking me and telling how she went home and prayed for forgiveness. She described the feelings she had and she thought she had been forgiven. "Could this really happen so quickly?" she wrote. I called her that night and asked her to come and see me Sunday. We both used the "year's supply" of tissue Sunday as we shared similar, sacred experiences.

The immediate results from a prayer and blessing happened when Karl fell off his bike and hit his head on the cement curb. The bump on his head was like those to which our family have become accustomed. A few days later, as we loaded the motor home for a trip to Yellowstone, I checked his black and blue bump while we were rushing to leave before the freeways became jammed. We then stopped for family prayer. Afterwards, both Sondra and I felt uneasy about Karl. We drove the over-loaded motor home to our pediatrician's office and waited for him to check Karl. The doctor penetrated the bump, cleaned away the blood and found a hole about the size of a quarter in Karl's scalp penetrating to the skull. His head was bandaged, I anointed and sealed, and we were on our way with the assurance that Karl would be all right. Had he participated in the activities we had planned he might not have completed the trip.

Time to Heal

Answers to blessings or prayers may be as immediate as the one Karl received, but usually they take time. My dear friends, Jim and Janet Wright, were ecstatic over the birth of a baby girl. Viewing this wide-eyed, round-faced little girl with locks of black velvet hair made me even sadder because the doctors thought she would soon die. She had been born with a defective kidney which was removed. Four months later it was necessary to remove some of her intestinal track. Now, with 90 percent of her small intestines removed she was having difficulty staying alive. I was there to assist the father in giving a blessing so the baby would live.

After sealing the anointing and being prompted by the Spirit, I promised the tiny, sleeping infant with all the priesthood authority we possessed that she would live, that she would be beautiful, and that she would bring great joy to her family and friends. Much more was promised. As I left the hospital I felt good about the blessing but the worries of the day had taken their toll on her parents. A sensitive home teacher, Gordon Mauss, gave them a special blessing to help them through this ordeal.

During this baby's first year of life, she was operated on eight times. She was not expected to live, but by the age of four she no longer needed the medication originally prescribed for a lifetime. Connie is all that was promised and more, but the healing of her body took time.

Sometimes there are both recognizable, immediate results and long-term results from a blessing. Our sixteen-month-old boy, adorable Mark, was the last child I kissed as I hurried out the back door to go to work. A mile from the house I saw, in my rear-view mirror, our van speed up behind me. "What is wreckless-driving Michael doing following me when he should be taking the van full of children to school?" I said out loud.

He pulled up beside me. Pale and upset Michael told me that Mark had followed me to my car and when I shut the garage door it had cut off his thumb. "All right," I said, unbelievably calm. "Everything will be okay. Take the children to school." I made an abrupt U-turn and sped home. Blood was all over the kitchen. Our Cambodian friend was trying to hold Mark as the blood spurted from his thumb. Sondra was attempting to stop the bleeding. The children still at home were becoming hysterical.

I said, "Everyone calm down, everything is going to be all right." With the bleeding stopped, I went to get the consecrated oil while I prayed for guidance. Mark pierced my anointing and sealing prayer with high-pitched cries. He was promised that his thumb would be healed—even restored— with no disfigurement. He stopped crying and was calm as we rushed to Long Beach Memorial Hospital.

The dangling top part of his thumb that had been severed by the weather-stripping on the garage door was sewn back on. We took him home to a night of throbbing pain but even when the attached thumb turned black we did not worry.

After several weeks of care by the hand surgeon, his thumb was whole. We can hardly tell now which thumb was injured. The blessing had immediate effect but it took time to see the results and—in this incident—a relatively short time to complete the healing process.

Long-Term Good

It sometimes takes many years for a prayer or blessing to be answered, or for us to fully understand the answer. It was fifteen years after my "Sports Point" prayer before I realized the full impact of that tearful night. The results of another prayer offered in my youth are still amazing to me. I was sixteen years old when I confronted my father with "Why can't the Negro hold the priesthood?" He tried to explain, but I was upset and could not understand. After all, I was the only Caucasian on our ninth grade basketball team. My father saw that I was visibly troubled and he suggested I pray about the matter. The effects of that sincere prayer took twenty-eight years to gradually unfold and they will probably continue forever.

I was accustomed to the common short prayer of asking for this and thanking for that. I really wanted to understand why Negroes were restricted from the priesthood after they joined the Church. I prayed, waited for an answer, and prayed again. After a few days of this, I still did not understand but I knew there was a reason. The Church's teaching no longer bothered me except when I would overhear someone discuss the Church's policy and a comment would be made that showed prejudice.

While I was the supervising elder of the Sheffield District, Governor Orville Fabus had his famous confrontation, in 1957, with the federal marshalls at Little Rock High School, in Arkansas. Every magazine and newspaper in England, where I was, showed whites beating Blacks and Blacks resisting. When my missionary companion and I used our door approach "We are ministers from America . . ." some people would interrupt us to say, "Why don't you go home and preach in Little Rock?"

At this same time *Look* magazine had favorable coverage on the "Mormons." Their article said, "All worthy males at the age of twelve years may be ordained to the priesthood, except the Negroes." Investigators and recent converts besieged the missionaries for answers to this apparent impasse. My companion and I fasted, prayed, and studied about this subject. Our lesson "Restrictions on the Priesthood" became an extra missionary lesson.

I have given this lesson over a hundred times and never had a problem. The last few times I gave it was on assignment from the Long Beach East Stake President. I spoke to a youth fireside group in every ward. "Busing" was a favorite topic of youth in the mid-1970s. Before ending my talk with a discussion of "Prejudice Doesn't Make Sense" I would bear my testimony germinating from prayers when I was sixteen—how I knew through my studies, the writings of prophets, and my own personal conviction that someday soon a prophet would say something like, "Now is the time to fellowship all brethren in the Priesthood of God." A week after I completed the last of the eight youth firesides, on June 9, 1978, someone called the secretary at our store and said, "Have you heard . . . ?" As the others sought more information and speculated excitedly about President Spencer W. Kimball's announcement that the blacks could now hold the priesthood I closed my office door and wept!

A week later, as a long-time black member of the Church spoke to our Young Adult fireside, neither he nor we could control our emotions. What a glorious feeling it was to realize that my youthful prayer had enabled me to help others with similar questions. Long-term good does come from fervent prayer.

The sensitivity I gained toward minorities through a teenager's prayer helped me in the community, too. As a school board member I led out in a well-planned voluntary integration effort. As chaos raged in bordering Los Angeles School District with its court-ordered, forced busing, we quietly established community-approved magnets. No white flight. All other large school districts in California were court mandated to alleviate racial isolation. There are no court orders in Long Beach, no over-crowded schools, no schools closing. Voluntary busing in California's fourth largest district solved a host of problems faced by other districts.

I am not taking credit for what has been termed "The finest integration program in the country." Hundreds of good people have made it successful. However, without the answer to my troubled, youthful prayer and the compassion learned from years of talking about prejudice, I would not have been as concerned or as outspoken as I was. The Lord answers prayers and uses us in "strange and mysterious ways, his wonders to perform."

Patience and long suffering are needed as we await the results of some blessings or complete answers to prayers. With a new and energetic missionary companion, Elder Brent Brockbank, we two elders went to work. We saturated Barnsley, England, with Books of Mormon. We often fasted and prayed. After three months we stood wet and bone-cold late at night waiting for the double-decker red bus with our arms overflowing with returned Books of Mormon. Since there was no place to sit down we leaned against a lamp post from sheer exhaustion. It was bitterly cold. Elder Brockbank turned to me and said, "What have we accomplished the past three months?" I asked him, "Would you rather have been home during summer vacation, or here?" "Here," he said, and I asked "Why?" Together we listed a good number of reasons. A month later the Ellison family, schoolteachers, were baptized after they decided to sell his 1938 Bently convertible so they could pay tithing. We elders then added patience to our list of reasons along with answer to prayer.

Occasionally the answers to our blessings and prayers not only takes time but comes in an unexpected manner. From the perspective of the present we can see the long-term good of past experience.

Learn from Suffering

Are we supposed to suffer? How can we know joy without sorrow? "For it must needs be, that there is an opposition in all things. If not so . . . righteousness could not be brought to pass, neither wickedness, neither holiness nor misery, neither good nor bad." (2 Nephi 2:11.) In depression, sickness, and death there is, seemingly, injustice. It is possible from heartache and physical difficulties to grow in "knowledge and stature." The Lord revealed to the Prophet Joseph Smith, while he was a prisoner in Liberty Jail in 1838, "If thou art called to pass through tribulation . . . know thou, my son, that all these things shall give thee experience, and shall be for thy good." When beset by all manner of tribulations, read all of section 122 of the Doctrine and Covenants.

President Harold W. Hoopes of the Los Angeles California Mission suffered physically without many of his missionaries knowing that he did. He and his devoted wife also gave constant care to their seriously ill daughter. Their suffering gave them unique qualities of love and compassion. The Apostle Paul gave another reason why some are buffeted: "And lest I should be exalted above measure through the abundance of the revelations, there was given to me a thorn in the flesh . . ." (2 Cor. 12:7).

After ten years of marriage, Sondra noticed a hearing loss. After testing, it was recommended that she have a hearing aid for her right ear. I blessed her to have her full hearing restored. As she became frustrated at not being able to hear soft-spoken conversations, the hearing aid was fitted in her ear. She now has them in both ears. Where is the answer to her prayers? Why has the blessing not "come to pass"? The blessing was more than a cure for her ailment. The Lord gave counsel and comfort. She was to benefit from her plight. In our noisy home she can turn down—or off—most sound. At night she slumbers as I am awakened by every sound. Her handicap is mostly a blessing. Sondra feels good about the blessings pronounced upon her ears. She is comfortable in conversations. She has faith that the Lord's will is being done. After her most recent hearing test showed improvement in both ears, Sondra said, "The doctors were amazed!" She knows the blessing will take time for her benefit.

Some righteous people are bedridden for years even after blessings promise good health. They may even reach the point of saying "My God, my God, why hast thou forsaken me?" (Matt. 27:46.) Each person and illness is different. The reasons for suffering vary. For some it is necessary to improve slowly, to learn about their bodies, to insure long-term recovery. Others may be "tried and tested." "God having provided some better things for them through their sufferings, for without sufferings they could not be made perfect." (JST, Heb. 11:40.) In time the blessings will "come to pass" if it is God's will.

During the summer before my senior year at BYU, five of us left from Holbrook, Arizona, to visit church sites and attend a student leadership conference. Sleeping on the muddy Hill Cumorah near Palmyra, New York, after the pageant was almost impossible because Hurricane Diane had struck. In the morning a testimony meeting in the Sacred Grove began with the sun's rays bouncing off droplets of water on the yellow-green leaves. A sister in a wheelchair bore her testimony about extraordinary sacrifices and how her handicap had blessed her life and others. Then the rains came. In sheets it rained and the testimony meeting went on and on. Californians do not carry umbrellas. I was still wet from the night before so I stayed. I was near the last to shake hands with Elder Adam S. Bennion, my mother's cousin. He asked about Mother and then I asked a dumb question: "Why would the Lord allow it to rain so hard during this testimony meeting?" Scowling, appearing irritated that a purported relative could ask such a question, he said, "You have suffered little here compared to your ancestors who crossed the plains, faced starvation in the Salt Lake Valley, and died so you could be here today." "Oh" I said, as he turned to the next person in line. (Sometimes we learn the hard way, but we do learn.)

Our trip ended, and as we came over the Rockies and looked down into the great Salt Lake Valley, I remembered Horace Greeley's description when he viewed the valley for the first time: "Bright, blistering, blinding, sterility." What we saw after two generations of hard work and suffering by our ancestors and thousands of others was a desert that blossomed like a rose.

In Joseph Smith's journal for August 6, 1842, we read: "I prophesied that the Saints would continue to suffer much affliction and would be driven to the Rocky Mountains, many would apostatize, others would be put to death by our persecutors or lose their lives in consequence of exposure or disease, and some of you will live to go and assist in making settlements and build cities and see the Saints become a mighty people in the midst of the Rocky Mountains." (*The Restored Church*, p. 252.) The answers to prayer and the fulfillment of prophecy took time, work, and suffering. It was the suffering of the early Saints I learned about that made this trip so satisfying. The stones in life that knocked them down were stepping stones to new achievements. They must have found great joy in their hard, but successful, struggle.

Set New Goals

Tragedy brings with it the challenge of rearranging life and setting new goals. In a talk to the graduating seniors of Lakewood High School's Class of '82, I reminded them of good-looking Jim Kanub who spoke at an assembly when they were sophomores. He had been a star pole-vaulter while he was a student at Lakewood High. He was on his way to the Olympic tryouts when an accident left him paralyzed from the waist down. His new goal was to walk. When that was impossible his goal was to win a local 10K wheelchair race. He had told the sophomores he planned to someday win the Boston Wheelchair Marathon. I announced to the graduates that he had just achieved that goal. They cheered! A tragedy may benefit a life after inspired changes are made.

The Lord allows accidents and seeming injustices to be part of life. We, who give blessings, should be cautious as we attempt to restore health. Some need assurance and motivation to overcome their handicap rather than to have full restoration of body or faculty. Listen carefully for the promptings of the Spirit.

We had a darling little girl in our ward who was retarded. It was a privilege to give her a blessing when she was ill. From observing her family, I learned about the parents' love, joy, and hardship in caring for her.

Our school district acquired the Buffum School for severely handicapped. Since I had visited our district's schools for the handicapped several times I was prepared somewhat for the visit. Children who lay in their specially formed beds at school and could only blink and open their mouths were heartbreaking. In this school were over one hundred children, most of whom were loved and who lived at home. A few were completely abandoned by parents but the parents I met shared their ordeal and love as they described the process of accepting, and then loving, a retarded child. Sitting with the dignitaries at our local Special Olympics I felt like honoring the parents as they cheered on their competing, beloved, special children.

The Lord permits accidents, injustice, tragedy and illness to occur. Who is to discern if it's God's will? The parents can with the help of fasting, prayer, blessings, priesthood counsel, and receiving their own personal revelation. Whatever the reasons, lives are changed and progress becomes the goal.

Illness caused me to reexamine my goals. In the spring of 1977, at the age of forty-three, my right ear developed a constant "stuffed" sensation and I had dizzy spells. Try playing tennis with the court in motion. Everyone was beating me. I was thoroughly checked. The doctors shook their heads and, in desperation, I went to bed. Being alone in the house gave me an opportunity to talk to God. I prayed for his healing influence morning, noon and night. After a week the prayers were less frequent, but a few were lengthy as in years past. I began to wonder if the Lord was trying to get my attention. I felt helpless and dependent upon Him.

In analyzing my position in life compared to my goals, I got out a worn college term paper. After the experience of "Sports Point" I had a statistics class my junior year at BYU. I chose, as my term project, to chart-plan my life in all areas. Taking the project seriously, I even fasted and prayed over a school assignment. Everything projected had come to pass earlier than planned, except marriage. It now dawned on me that everything except after-death goals had been accomplished. It was time to set new goals in order to productively strive and keep life interesting.

From direct answer to prayer and another blessing given by my brothers, Sondra and I made the following decisions: (1) have another child; (2) run for the local school board the next year; (3) await a call to serve as a counselor to the full-time mission president; and (4) repent of things in my life that did not seem totally right. With these decisions made I got better and went back into life's routine.

A week later I was called to share the high council assignment for the stake mission. President F. Britton McConkie arrived as the new president of the California Los Angeles Mission. In my stake mission capacity I requested of him two more missionaries. Besides, how could I become his counselor if we never met? Well, I did not ask to be his counselor, nor did he ask me. In the Lord's own time, I thought.

Three months later one of my children said, "A man with a deep voice wants to talk to you." The voice on the phone said, "This is President McConkie of the Los Angeles Mission. We've never met, but I would like you to assist me in this mission." I said, "I would be glad to." He had not asked me to be his counselor, but I knew that is what he meant. Then on March 20, 1978, I was elected to the Board of Education of the Long Beach Unified School District and three days later John Allen entered our family—healthy, happy and such a joy.

There are many reasons for suffering. Every life is different. It is important to try to understand the reasons. It is extremely important to learn to care for ourselves before, during, and after an illness. The major point is that we do not have to suffer physically, mentally, or spiritually as much or as long after we have a priesthood blessing.

VI

Conditions for an Effectual Blessing

The results of a blessing may be immediate or it may take time. More important is whether or not the blessing will be effectual. It will, depending on four conditions: first, faith of the individual receiving the blessing; second, faith of the person giving the blessing; third, priesthood authority; and fourth, God's will.

Faith of the Receiver

Faith in God

Many people are healed daily by their faith in God. All nations, kindred, tongues and people can heal themselves through faith. The woman who followed behind Jesus Christ said to herself, If I may touch his garment, I shall be whole. The Savior told her, "Daughter, be of good comfort; thy faith hath made thee whole" (Matt. 9:21-22).

On one occasion I rushed to the hospital because the ward Relief Society president had been admitted a few hours earlier with a serious illness. I found her sitting up, smiling. "Hurry up, give me a blessing so I can get out of here!" she said. There was probably no need for the blessing her husband and I gave her. This righteous woman may have already healed herself by her own faith; or, more properly, God had healed her before our arrival because of her faith in Him and the priesthood. "He who hath faith to see shall see. He who hath faith to hear shall hear. The lame who hath faith to leap shall leap." (D&C 42:49-51.)

A home teacher asked me to join him in blessing an inactive sister. As their bishop, I knew the family and their problems well. This middle-aged mother had struggled with many of life's problems and now she had learned that she had cancer. She described her cancer in a strangely resigned manner. She did not ask for a blessing. Thinking she might be hesitating because of family members present or because she felt unworthy I said, "We have come prepared to give you a blessing if you desire one." She seemed to think about it, then she said, "Well, I don't know what good it would do now, but go ahead."

The home teacher anointed with oil and I sealed the anointing. I was impressed to pray about the family's need to have her live. She was promised good health. She was to exercise her faith to know the healing power of the Lord. As soon as I said, "In the name of Jesus Christ, Amen," she said, "Bishop, I've written down instructions for my funeral."

Her home teacher and I tried to be positive and buoy her up to ". . . succor the weak, lift up the hands which hang down, and strengthen the feeble knees" (D&C 81:5). But as we walked away from the house I sorrowfully commented, "Brother, she is going to die—and she doesn't need to." He said, with sadness, "I know." She was going to die, not because it was God's will, lack of authority, or our faith which now wavered, but because she wanted out—to be gone from life's many problems. She did not have faith to be healed.

This was an agonizing judgment for a young bishop to make and a hard funeral to conduct two months later. Even a person who believes a little can be helped. ". . . whosoever among you are sick, and have not faith to be healed, but believe, shall be nourished with all tenderness . . ." (D&C 42:43).

The faith of many may combine to heal the sick. Family and friends fast and pray and hundreds within the temple may add their faith.

One morning the question was asked, in our high priests quorum, "What significance does placing a name on the temple prayer rolls have in healing the sick?" A member of the quorum said, "Those going through the temple for their own or another's endowment add their faith and prayer for those whose names are upon the altar." The quorum's most diligent temple attender responded, "Those in the temple are the most faithful in the Church!" Another temple worker said, "During eight sessions daily hundreds of worthy brothers and sisters are concentrating on those names placed in the temple that day," and he suggested that an ill person should know the day their name is placed in the temple.

For two months my sister was seriously ill. Doctors, medication, blessings or temple prayers had not yet reversed her bodily deterioration. Her family was frantic as she "wasted away." Her symptoms ceased the Sunday her ward prayed and fasted for her.

The combined effect of personal supplication, priesthood blessings, temple prayers, and group fasts produces the faith that can cause dramatic miracles. For some, all that is necessary is their own faith in God which is sufficient to be healed. Family, priesthood and temple prayers are an aid to the sick in approaching the faith of a grain of a mustard seed (Matt. 17-20) that removes mountains.

Faith and Works

In September of 1980, I had been sluggish. Excessive thirst and a salty taste in my mouth would have warned a more knowledgeable person that something was wrong. I finally went to a doctor for a checkup. Three days later 2,000 teachers filled Lakewood High School's auditorium to vent their views on the board's collective bargaining proposals. Afterwards, I went home ill and was still too ill the next morning to go to work. The doctor called me. He said, "The results of the tests show your blood sugar is six times normal! I want you in the hospital today for treatment of diabetes."

I got out the medical encyclopedia and read about the pancreas failing to make insulin. I called my brothers, Bob and Craig, who blessed me to totally recover. *The World Book Encyclopedia* stated: "Diabetes cannot be cured. But the disease can be controlled by injections of insulin and careful attention to diet."

For the first time since birth I was admitted to a hospital; this time to be treated for severe adult onset diabetes. For ten days I was given injection after injection of insulin.

Sondra came into my stuffy hospital room one smoggy afternoon crying. "What's wrong?" I worried. "Oh, I'm just trying to decide between you and sugar," she said. Fortunately, she went home and gave away all our sugar products. The family had decided to live my diet—at home, anyway. Sondra bought a years supply of syringes.

I rotated the insulin shots from arms, thighs, and stomach. Balancing the insulin and food intake was hard. If not properly done my body would go out-of-whack. After a month and a half of struggling and praying I said to Sondra, "I have had it! I'm going to bring these shots to an end!"

We plotted to gradually reduce the amount of insulin until December when I would stop. I was to exercise my "gift of faith" and "gift to be healed" contained in my patriarchal blessing. The blessing I received said "totally well" which for me did not include insulin shots. My prayers were more determined: "Show me what diet, what exercise to follow." The faith to get well had materialized. Faith, however, was not enough. ". . . shew me thy faith without thy works, and I will shew thee my faith by my works" (James 2:18).

The doctor checked my progress and in December, 1980, I told him I was off insulin. He wished me luck and set up advance appointments. Sondra gave away the needles. In section 89 of my Doctrine and Covenants I have written, in big red letters, "NO SUGAR!—LOW FAT!" This section has become so much more meaningful to our family. There are so many fad diets. "Lo here!" and others "Lo there!" ". . . I often said to myself: What is to be done? Who of all these parties are right; . . ." (JST, 2:5, 10.) "If any of you lack wisdom let him ask of God . . ." (James 1:5). The answer to my prayer on this matter is always, "Read again section 89."

I abused my body by not reading further than "strong drinks, tobacco, and hot drinks." Why didn't I follow the teachings about "Wholesome herbs . . . fruit in the season . . . flesh of beasts and of the fowls . . . used sparingly . . . only in times of winter, or of cold, or famine . . . all grain . . . to be the staff of life . . . is good for the food of man; . . . as that which yieldeth fruit whether in the ground or above the ground . . . all saints who remember to keep and do these sayings . . . shall receive health . . . the destroying angel shall pass by them. . . ." There is so much contained within these few verses. A knowledge of diet makes this scripture more meaningful. I believe moderation in eating meat and increased use of whole grains, vegetables, and some fruit will bless my family and me the rest of our earthly lives. Good again comes from adversity.

I had everything going for me; faith, the faith of my family, "gift to be healed," priesthood authority and God's will, but until I started putting forth "works" I was insulin-dependent. My faith is that I must try to live all of section 89 as well as exercise to remain insulin free. That is my part in God's total healing of me. With my doctor's OK I have torn up my diabetic ID card.

Faith of the Giver

Positive Faith

The persons who give a blessing must have sufficient faith. ". . . if you have not faith, hope and charity you can do nothing" (D&C 18:19). My bishopric counselor, who was the home teacher to frail Sister Dills, invited me to assist him in giving her a blessing. She was the ward's most elderly sister. When we entered her musty, paper-strewn room, she complained of old age and being resigned to death. Brother Johansen blessed her with more years of life. She had genealogy to do! After he said, "Amen," he added, "Time to get up." We helped her out of bed and sat her in the desk chair. Brother "J" gathered up the genealogy sheets and helped her sort them. He, along with the visiting teachers, cleaned her house the next day. She proudly showed them, on their weekly visits, her genealogy accomplishments. The faith and works of her home teacher helped her faith and kept this delightful sister alive for many years.

The faith of the person giving the blessing may be as important as the faith of the person receiving the blessing. The Lord said, ". . . whoso shall ask it in my name in faith, they shall cast out devils; they shall heal the sick; . . ." (D&C 35:9).

When Jesus was beseeched by a centurion to heal his tormented servant ". . . Jesus saith unto him, I will come and heal him." The centurion showed great faith when he said, "I am not worthy that thou shouldest come under my roof: but speak the word only and my servant shall be healed." Jesus said to the centurion ". . . as thou hast believed, so be it done unto thee. And his servant was healed in the selfsame hour." (Matthew 8:5-13.) We should be positive and exercise faith as we go forth to use the healing power of the priesthood.

My faith combined with others may have extended a life. During the historic fires in Northridge, California, in 1971, Sister Martin and her son, Paul, were visiting relatives. Her little redheaded, blue-eyed, three-year-old son, Paul, wandered outside and fell into the swimming pool. Sister Martin, sensing something wrong, found him, rescued him from the pool and gave mouth-to-mouth resuscitation until the paramedics arrived. The home teacher, Bill Williams, and I hurriedly drove to the Northridge Hospital. I loved the Martin family. The father, Jim, and I were tennis opponents and he had recently been baptized. Karen was a devoted, intelligent mother. In the busy Intensive Care ward we met our worried, humbled friends. Paul was in a coma. He was hooked up to life support and monitoring systems. He was not expected to live. The doctors and nurses stepped aside and in the now silent ward Bill anointed and I pleaded with the Lord to let beautiful Paul live. If there was ever a time to use the power of the priesthood, this was it. The words came: "You will live . . . your parents will understand the purpose of this accident. . . ."

Paul remained in a coma as he was transferred to UCLA Medical Center and then to the Primary Childrens Hospital in Salt Lake City. Those who cared for him fell in love with Paul's "heavenly countenance." Our ward and the church congregations of Paul's relatives fasted and prayed. Eventually Paul was placed in Fairview Hospital in Costa Mesa, California, where the parents and friends could visit regularly. Seeing the dozens of children returning to a fetal position as they lay in a deep coma made me less critical of my own active children.

Eight years later there was no indication that the spirit was about to leave Paul's earthly body. But at the age of eleven Paul's spirit was free of his handicapped body. I gave the eulogy at the funeral and told about the parents bringing their two sons into the bishop's office for a name and a blessing. Of those present some remember only vaguely (others remember vividly) that Paul was told he would not suffer; that he would be spared the trials in life others must suffer.

Looking back on this experience I believe my faith and the faith of many was a factor in Paul living for seven more years. "For what purpose?" has been asked. The blessing said the parents would understand. I prayed that "God's will would be done."

Lack of Faith

My lack of faith may have been part of the reason a person died. This experience is difficult for me to tell. A customer called our furniture store and asked for Bishop Ward. She was presently not active in the Church. Her husband was not a member and he was going to have open-heart surgery the next morning. His wife was worried and she believed a blessing would help. We were the only "Mormons" she was able to contact. Reluctantly, I asked the salesmen, "Who will go with me to give a blessing?" and Dave Terry volunteered.

I worry to this day if perhaps I went begrudgingly. At the hospital, the middle-aged healthy-looking man was in high spirits. I am not sure he expected our visit. He was cordial as I explained anointing and sealing. The ward was open and several patients and nurses listened or watched. We could only partially draw the curtain around us and the T.V. blared from above the adjoining bed. We stretched awkwardly over the bed's cold metal side-bars to reach his head. I was so aware of the uncomfortable, noisy surroundings I could not remember what was said in the blessing. It seemed mechanical. He thanked us and I could feel the people in the hospital ward staring at us as we left. Perhaps because I was feeling a little guilty I called the hospital the next day to ask how the patient was doing. He had died on the operating table.

Had my lack of faith . . . (I don't want to ask the question). I will not know in this life. I do know I have since been better prepared—not lacking in faith.

Develop Confidence

The person who is receiving a blessing should have confidence in the person who is giving a blessing. It took several years of marriage before my wife gradually gained confidence in my ability to give blessings. For the past fifteen years she has not hesitated. She has witnessed, many times, the immediate and long-term effects of numerous blessings. Only once, for a brief time, shortly after our marriage, did she lose confidence in me.

In the silent early-morning hours, Sondra sat up in bed wide awake in terror as I yelled while thrashing about the bed. The high-pitched sounds coming from me as I clutched my leg caused her to burst into helpless tears. After a couple of minutes of horror and with a great deal of courage she reached out to me and sobbed, "Honey, what's wrong?" I went silently limp. "What's wrong?" she repeated and turned on the light. In a calm, sleepy voice I said, "What do you mean what's wrong; nothing is wrong. Go back to sleep."

She sat there frozen against the headboard. Sondra, by now, was frightened of me, her normal rock of support. There I was, pretending nothing was wrong after screaming loudly in the middle of the night. When she tried to tell me what happened, she became worried about herself and the children because I told her it was she who was having a nightmare. As I turned over to hug her, she jerked back. "Don't touch me!" I was now fully awake and worried about Sondra's nocturnal actions. The more I reasoned with her about her nightmare the more upset she became. In attempting to get out of bed I fell flat on my face. My leg had collapsed.

Talking about it in the early morning we figured out what happened. During my sound sleep a charley horse developed in my leg and I screamed from the pain. As the charley horse went away, Sondra had awakened me, but I had no knowledge or symptom of the leg pain until I tried to stand. Even with this explanation, Sondra was leery of me for several days. She had very little confidence in me. If a priesthood bearer were to give a blessing to a person who does not have confidence in him, he may neutralize the faith of that person.

As the years pass and numerous blessings are given in our homes, our families develop faith in our ability to bless them, faith in the priesthood, and faith in God. On March 16, 1981, Sondra wrote in her journal, "John and I celebrated our 18th anniversary . . . He has honored and magnified his priesthood to the point where I have no doubt that he could heal me with the Lord's power from any disease. The Lord has cured me, through him, of my allergies, back problems, and many minor illnesses. I am blessed . . ." Sondra has great faith in God, in me, in priesthood authority and in God's will being done. No wonder blessings given to her restore her health almost immediately.

Priesthood Authority

Priesthood authority is an important factor in performing an ordinance acceptable to God. Giving credit to Jesus Christ and God the Father and sustaining priesthood leadership is vital as we perform our priesthood duties. Numerous healings are attempted by persons with no priesthood authority.

Power of Satan

Sometimes switching channels between television commercials, my family and I will watch church services where people are being healed. Our favorite is a man who hits them on the forehead with his open hand or smacks their ears and says "Heal!" and they appear healed. We oft-times discuss these performed episodes as a family. Yes, faith can heal these people—so can Satan who causes much of the illness in the world. Satan will heal the body in order to destroy the soul. "By what authority doest thou these things? and who gave thee this authority?" (Matt. 21:23.) Satan will use the appearance of authority, truth and good to obstruct the Lord's work.

Satan has used devious tactics to maintain pornography in our neighborhood. As co-chairman of "Citizens Against X-rated Movies at the Lakewood Theatre" my responsibility was to supervise the picketing of over 400 people at the theater. The purpose of the picketing was to get media coverage: thus, the attention of the community and its leaders. It was probably the first time many of these well-dressed neighborhood people, and my older children, had carried a picket sign. We felt that we were getting our message across to the television, radio and press reporters when a yellow van drove up. The van was covered with phrases and symbols. The loud speaker cried "Repent sinners." Out got husky men carrying 5-foot by 7-foot canvas signs stating "Burn in Hell" and "Repent or Perish." The media turned to them. We who had worked so hard in planning a mature, calm event, gasped. We tried to reason with the demonstrators from the van but they pushed their way into our picket lines. Our neighbors began to drift away, one saying, "I'll have no part of this." We called off the picketing early. Guess what appeared in the media? The theater had their good-looking, calm, reasonable public relations man interviewed on T.V. The "balanced" reporting showed a wild-eyed giant carrying the "Burn in Hell" sign. If these people are sincere in their efforts, do they realize the harm they do?

Satan's influence can gradually entwine itself in the lives of honest, unsuspecting people as evidenced by the following dramatic story.

After my wife had her hair done at a nearby beauty salon, she came home one day asking about Ouija boards. Her hairdresser was getting answers—"good vibes"—while playing the game. I told Sondra that her hairdresser might be taking the playful part of the game into dangerous territory. Sondra discussed with her my concern, but the hairdresser was now getting a voice response to the questions she posed during the game. I suggested to Sondra that she might want to change hairdressers. She agreed. The next appointment was to be her last.

After she had her hair done, Sondra, a little frightened, rushed to our store. Her hairdresser had received a revelation. We were supposed to light candles, read passages in the Book of Revelation and join her and her husband in Hawaii to meet Christ.

At first I jokingly said, "You will try anything to go to Hawaii." Sondra was not amused and she never again went to that hairdresser. A month later, the hairdresser called Sondra asking for help. She had gone to a minister seeking guidance and he did not believe her story. We were the only "religious people" she knew. Her first clue that something might be wrong was when her sixteen-year-old niece, who was living with her, began writing under the direction of her uncle who was dead. The niece, with the spirit of her uncle moving her hand, had written that she no longer had to attend high school. The hairdresser wanted me to come and help them.

When Sondra handed the phone to me, with a worried look, I had the strangest sensation go through my body. Always, I have tried to respond immediately to cries for help, but this time I told the hairdresser I would think about it and call her back. At work I asked the stake president, President Zimmerman, what I should do. The hairdresser was not a member of the Church, so it came under the missionary program. The stake missionary in the Long Beach Second Ward, in which boundaries she resided, was my huge, gentle friend, Frank Johnson.

When I called the hairdresser back to set up an appointment for us that evening, she mentioned the "spirit" inhabiting their apartment. Waiting for Frank in my car near her apartment, I found the scripture where Satan appears as an angel of light. ". . . Satan himself is transformed into an angel of light. Therefore it is no great thing if his ministers also be transformed as the ministers of righteousness; . . ." (2 Cor. 11:14-15.) When Frank arrived we had a solemn prayer together before going up the stairs to the woman's apartment. We had both faced situations similar to this in the mission field. In fact Frank had made a study of Satanic religions. When the hairdresser opened the door I expected all hell to break loose. Instead this lovely young woman welcomed us and introduced us to an equally lovely niece. She told us the "spirit" had just told them that we were men of God and that they should listen to us. I felt we were being set up. I thought, What next?

We sat around a small table in the close, dimly lit living room. There were dark circles beneath their swollen, red eyes. Other than that they were attractive young ladies. The hairdresser started telling us in detail about what had taken place during the past month. I interrupted her unusual and fascinating story, even though I wanted to hear more, because I felt we were being led someplace we should not go. I told them, with conviction, that it was Satan and his evil spirits who were leading them to do wrong things. They interrupted and showed us the niece's pile of scribbled writings. Her dead uncle had somehow taken control of her arm and hand. She would write mysterious directives for hours. The niece said, "Would you like to see me do it?" She was disappointed when I said, "No!" Frank read some of her writings as I explained to them Matthew 7:22-23: "Many will say to me in that day, Lord, Lord, have we not prophesied in thy name? and in thy name have we not cast out devils? and in thy name done many wonderful works? And then will I profess unto them, I never knew you: depart from me, ye that work iniquity."

Frank pushed a paper in front of me. It said, "You and John Ward are to remake the earth." I felt the same bodily sensation I had when I talked on the phone. Frank told me later that there were more pages about the hairdresser, Sondra, and me, but all I read was that one sentence. Frank and I bore our testimonies, we knelt, and we commanded—by the power of the priesthood and in the name of Christ—that the evil one depart the premises and the lives of the women.

We left. Frank and his missionary companion taught them the discussions until the hairdresser left to join her husband at his military station. As far as I know, they had no more contact with evil spirits.

What would have happened if Sondra had become more involved with her hairdresser? She was laying hands on Sondra's head, giving her blessings as she did her hair. What if I had made that visit to the hairdresser's apartment alone? What if Frank and I had allowed ourselves to become intrigued with the details of supernatural events? What if we had allowed a demonstration of their writing or communication skills? We could have been trapped and fallen fast. The following week I was called to the Long Beach Stake High Council. Frank was later called to be a bishop. Were we set up? I believe so, but by following proper procedure and inspiration it backfired on Satan. "Resist the devil, and he will flee from you" (James 4:7).

Notice in this story how Satan uses truth, Christ's name, blessings, and good, unsuspecting people to further his plan. When I found some of the youth in the Lakewood Second Ward playing with Ouija boards, guess what personal experience I told them?

Power of the Priesthood

My father, Karl Ward, tells several stories in his journal of how he was healed by the power of the priesthood. He gives credit to priesthood authority, faith, and personal prayer. His long-term healing by God's recognized representatives on earth is in stark contrast to the unauthorized short-term healers parading on the electronic media.

He recorded:

> At 10 years of age I was stricken with awful typhoid fever and was bed ridden for months and months. I lost my hair and had to learn to walk all over again. The elders administered to me and promised me that I would live a good and long life. My doctor, Brother William, just graduated from Columbia Medical School, and came to my bedside. He said, "Feed this boy." The country doctor had said, "Starve a fever." I am so thankful for this good brother's advice because he helped the elders' promise come true.

My father also wrote in his life's story:

> Art, Angus and I, one warm spring day, went swimming in Harding's pond. Angus and I were crossing the pond to get our clothes on the other side. He could swim but I couldn't. I stepped into a hole and nearly drowned. Art, who was now dressed, dashed in with his clothes on and pulled me out. He tried to jossle [sic] the water out of my lungs, but I fainted. They carried me home, and father again blessed me, and after ten days in bed I lived. Was it luck, chance, or did it just happen?

After sharing many other priesthood healings my father wrote:

> Thanks to the great healing power among all these faithful priesthood members . . . No it wasn't just luck or chance; it was the great faith, wearing of the garments, and power of the Holy Ghost together with my own personal prayers that pulled me through all of these dangerous situations.

Remember that long-term good comes from a priesthood blessing— from any act or ordinance performed properly with God's authority. To distinguish between good and evil is to recognize the guidance of the Spirit. "The Spirit beareth record" (D&C 58:24).

Will of God

The most important factor in being healed or receiving direction in our lives is the will of God. More than anything else we should want to do what we are foreordained to do—what God wants us to do.

Death of Children

God's will seems to be clearer to mankind as it pertains to children; "Jesus said, Suffer little children, and forbid them not, to come unto me: for of such is the kingdom of heaven. And he laid his hands on them . . ." (Matt. 19:14-15).

My mother's sister, Vernetta Lindsay Hodgson after having two sons waited five years before Richard was born at Long Beach Community Hospital in 1935. A best friend of Vernetta and Russell Hodgson was Dr. Nelson Young, their obstetrician. He had to tell Russell that, during birth, a blood clot went to his wife's brain and killed her. Elder John A. Widtsoe and Elder James E. Talmage spoke at her funeral. The child lived, and "Dickie" was an angelic child. Russell Hodgson remarried and moved to Ventura. A few years later Dr. Young and his wife stopped by to visit their friends. Afton Hodgson said, "You can't leave without seeing Dickie." He was asleep and she went in to awaken him. His spirit had left his body with no signs of struggle: he was still on his hands and knees, with a smile on his face.

My mother's sister, Lona Lindsay Heiner, also had a beautiful baby boy. She brought him to Long Beach to see if the lower altitude might help his heart condition. One night she called for my father to "minister to her baby." While he was administering to the child, my mother records in her journal: "I was watching and all of a sudden I saw him look up at the corner of the room and a beautiful smile came on his face. I knew someone had come to get him. It certainly strengthened my faith in a hereafter. When Karl finished the blessing he was dead."

Another child saw a heavenly being as he struggled between life and death four floors below my hospital room. I had just been placed in my room after two days in the Intensive Care ward. I was feeling sorry for myself. Open-heart surgery had sapped my physical and emotional strength. Dennis Rosenlof, good friend and handyman around our home, came to visit me. He sat down, asked how I was and began to cry. His six-year-old son, Todd, the "sweetest little kid that ever walked the earth," had that morning been admitted in a half-conscious condition. That night Todd was in a coma from Reyes Syndrome. His chances of living were fifty-fifty. Dennis blessed his son to live and said he "felt the presence of the Spirit." The bishop gave a blessing to Dennis and his wife, Robin—"This was something they had to go through"—and that "Todd would run and play again soon." Not only did I pray for myself and my family, I prayed for Todd and his family, as did the whole ward.

After eight days this delightful boy awoke. For another week he had difficulty communicating. When his parents first told him about prayers and blessings given on his behalf, he would cry and try to speak. When Dennis told him again later about the blessing he had given him, Todd said, "I know, Daddy, Jesus was standing right there holding my hand." Todd knew he would be taken care of. His recovery was complete. It was God's will.

Are we "appointed unto death?" (D&C 42:48.) The word of the Lord to the Prophet Joseph Smith was "Thy days are known, and thy years shall not be numbered less; therefore, fear not what man can do, for God shall be with you forever and ever." (D&C 122:9.)

As I rode with a member of the Sheffield district presidency to our "digs" in Doncaster, England, we talked about blessings. He had to pull to the side of the road to finish telling us about his precious daughter.

She was the only girl in the family—a sparkling, delightful "Daddy's girl." When she was five years old, she got pneumonia. Her father blessed her every day and the missionaries also blessed her to get well. After two months of the child getting no better and no worse he was desperate. He sought for missionaries who had the "gift to heal." They, too, commanded her to "rise up and walk." The father was overcome with grief as his little girl lay motionless. He held her feverish body and made covenants with God if she would only get better.

The mission president and a General Authority were visiting a distant district conference. The member of the district presidency implored them to come heal his daughter. He cried as he finished the story. The church leaders left their busy schedule and came to bless his little girl. Her head was anointed once again and as the father, the mission president, and several missionaries held his daughter, the General Authority prayed. He acknowledged all the prayers and blessings previously bestowed on the little girl. He said the Lord had heard their prayers and that God loved her, too. Then he said, "Now Father, we release her into thy hands. Let *thy will* be done." When they opened their eyes, hers had closed.

The passing of his child had taken place many years earlier, but his memory of that blessing was perfect. His loss was cushioned by the assurance that it was "God's will." He knows he will raise her in the resurrection if he continues to live righteously. It was obvious from the tears streaming down this father's cheeks that he missed his daughter very much.

The priesthood bearer, by diligent preparation, will know God's will by inspiration. If you perform with "unwearyingness," as did Nephi, the Lord has promised: ". . . thou shalt not ask that which is contrary to my will" (Helaman 10:5).

Plan of Salvation

Life takes unexpected turns. A knowledge of life's purpose softens life's blows and keeps us on course. Consider the tragic upheaval in the life of Jim and Tim Dunlap, who were waiting after priesthood meeting in Hemet, California, for their young wives and children to arrive for Sunday School.

Tim's wife, Lori, and teenage friend, Cindy, were in the car with Jim's pregnant wife, Linda, and their young boys, Ammon and Aaron, when their car was hit. The crash was an accident, a tragedy—or was it destiny? All were killed except for three-year-old Aaron.

Excerpts from the sermon I gave at their funeral sums up the Dunlaps' belief and mine concerning life and death—God's plan of salvation:

> After hearing the news we are stunned, unbelieving! Then there swells within a deep love and desire to help the families who mourn. But how? We cry, we pray, we awkwardly try to offer condolences. We would do anything to take away the hurt or bring them back.
>
> Yet at the time these families need our love and understanding, they have been the ones who have strengthened us.
>
> My goal in speaking is to have you feel as Jim and Tim and many others present; that is, a peace of mind that "all is well." No one can take away the sadness of being separated from a loved one for a time, but a peace within is also possible and necessary.
>
> May I tell you God's "Plan of Life and Death" in story form?
>
> Birth is not the beginning of life.
>
> Death is not the end of life.
>
> We lived before this earthlife as spirits with our Father in Heaven. We have a "Father of our spirit" (Heb. 12:9). We come to earth; a veil is drawn; Spirit and body unite. Christ told Nephi "On the morrow come I into the world" (3 Nephi 1:3). The following day he was a babe in his mother's arms.
>
> The purpose of earthlife is to:
>
> First gain a body, our prime purpose. It is all that is necessary for some. Others must prove themselves and gain experience "to see if we would do all things whatsoever the Lord our God shall command." We are to have joy and sorrow, ease and hardship, health and sickness, success and disappointments, and be tempted. We knew we must die. Before we came we accepted all eventualities willingly. We were eager to accept the favorable and the unfavorable. We wanted earthlife even though it might be for a day, year, or century. We were not concerned how we would die, whether by disease, accident, or heart attack.
>
> Death must come to all; it is one more step into eternity. When the spirit leaves the body, it enters the spirit world or in the case of Linda, Lori, Cindy, and Ammon, that portion called Paradise. Now is a busy time for them with reunions and learning. While Christ's body lay in the tomb for three days, his spirit was in Paradise too. Where is this spirit world? It is here on earth where their presence and possibly influence might be felt. They are not far from us. Possibly with us today.

Someday we will join our deceased loved ones in the spirit world. Or as young Jim Dunlap and I suddenly realized at the time of the resurrection, which is not far off.

Christ's spirit reentered a perfect body and when He appeared to His apostles they were ". . . terrified and affrighted, and supposed that they had seen a spirit." But Christ said unto them, ". . . handle me, and see; for a spirit hath not flesh and bones, as ye see me have." (Luke 24:37, 39.)

He was the first to be resurrected. So will all mankind during the millennium that follows Christ's second coming.

Surely Ammon, Cindy, Lori and Linda's spirits will be reunited with perfect celestial bodies the morning of the first resurrection. Families will be reunited; children will be resurrected as children and worthy parents will be allowed to rear them to maturity.

After all mankind has come forth in order of their faithfulness and the millennium ends, we then stand before God the Eternal Father to be judged. We face our life's record with all its story of our words, works, thoughts, and repentance; hopefully we will be found worthy to live again with God.

I can't judge, but after talking to those who can and learning more about Lori, Linda and Cindy, I feel they all deserve the highest glory possible. Of course, all children, as will Ammon, gain the highest, or celestial, kingdom.

I attended the wedding of Jim and Linda and Tim and Lori. They were not married "Till death do us part." They were married for "time and all eternity." I still remember the Spirit of the Lord's presence during the priesthood sealing of their marriage on earth and in heaven. Sometime in the future they—as husband and wife, as resurrected beings exalted in the celestial kingdom— may have spirit children. Under the tutorship of God and Jesus Christ after eons of time, they too may learn to create and become with their family part of the never-ending universe. And the plan of salvation, the circle of life, begins anew.

This life is but a brief moment in eternity, yet our most important! If viewed in perspective with eternity and future reuniting, it is easier to live this life. We should feel remorse, and rightly so. The separation seems so long. As Tim said, "I'm happy they are where they are, missing them will be the hardest thing."

Those who miss loved ones need help! As I spoke with Tim, he was concerned for Jim—Jim was concerned for Tim. These two husbands have their inspired partial answers as to why. So will all who study and seek their answer in humble prayer.

Our main concern should be: can we live lives good enough to be where they will be, the celestial kingdom? With the Lord's help and the help of one another, we can!

My brothers and sisters, the things I have told you have been taught by past and living prophets. I know them to be true!

We put our faith and trust in the Lord during trials like this that His will will be done ". . . in his own time, and in his own way, and according to his own will" (D&C 88:68). Viewed in relationship with the eternal plan, tragedies are softened and hope is offered.

A knowledge of God's plan of salvation aids us in understanding accidents, suffering, and God's will. Without this knowledge, people may agonize over death and illness, and blame God. A testimony of the gospel of Jesus Christ will eventually bring about peace and a positive feeling even during a tragedy. An elder can bless those suffering physically, emotionally, and spiritually during these occurrences. It is during times like this that a father/patriarch, priesthood leader, or home teacher is grateful for his preparation to be able to truly bless the grieved, the distraught, the lonely, the anguished and the needy.

VII

Epilogue: Open-Heart Surgery

I have wanted, for several years, to write about the need to ask for and give more blessings, but doubts about propriety and of my ability to write have caused me to postpone the completion of this book. Finally, the motivation and inspiration to finish began with a series of events in the fall of 1982.

Serving on the Long Beach Unified School District Board of Education, I became aware of the great need to reform public education at the state level. I also felt an intense desire to strengthen the family unit and to help persons with small businesses. After much prayer and discussion with family and friends, I considered running for a California state senate seat. It was time to file for reelection to the school board and since my plans were to run for the senate, I could not be elected again for a four-year term knowing I would seek a senate seat during that time. Several newspaper articles and editorials wished me success. (Two weeks later I was gerrymandered during a second reapportionment from my senate district into another where I would have to face a twenty-four-year incumbent senator of the same political party.)

Since my health would be a major factor in my future plans I had a complete physical. I was in good shape except for a treadmill stress test which indicated a possible problem, and then a nuclear scan showed—on a television monitor—that blood was not flowing out of my heart as fast as it should with exertion.

My doctor suggested a coronary angiogram where they probe into the arteries of the heart while they view a catheter's passage on a television monitor. I hesitated because of my aversion to someone probing around inside my body; besides, there would be no open-heart surgery for me—even if they found problems. I prayed to know what to do.

During a Christmas gathering of the stake presidents at the mission home, President Gerald Iba of the Santa Monica Stake shared his medical expertise and suggested I find out for sure if there was any arterial disease. This meant having the angiogram. My brothers later gave me a blessing before I entered the hospital.

I was sedated but conscious during the angiogram at Long Beach Memorial Hospital. I could see the monitors and feel some of the probing of the catheter. Comments made by the medical staff warned me, in my stupor, that something was wrong. Later that day, distressed and in tears, my wife entered the room with the doctor. They showed me a diagram of my heart. The three major arteries in my heart were blocked, 100 percent calcified on the right and over 80 percent on the left ones. Coronary artery disease had stopped the blood flow through most of the larger arteries of my heart. Only because of a "strong heart" had collateral circulation developed, keeping my heart alive and me from feeling pain. A serious heart attack was, in the doctor's opinion, imminent. But I felt great; there were no current symptoms; how could this be? Yet the doctors indicated my need for five or six bypasses.

Sondra cried; I cried later thinking about the seriousness of open-heart surgery, the future quality of life, the need to see my children grow and become secure in life. What could have caused the accumulation of plaque within my arteries? — I have never smoked or drank. How will my family and the business fare without me? How will Sondra cope with me incapacitated for months? What other alternatives are there to avoid this operation? I wondered. Wait a minute. I have the "gift to be healed" as stated in my patriarchal blessing.

Lying on my back in the unfamiliar hospital bed that night, my mind would not stop. I wept, prayed, and finally entered a drugged sleep. Sondra and I both knew that the operation scheduled for the next week was necessary. Our families were notified and they were exceptionally supportive. I told the staff of the school district and the editor of the Press Telegram that I would not file for reelection to the school board, but that I would seek a senate seat after I recovered from the surgery. They encouraged me to stay on the school board and they offered their help. Then the deputy superintendent said, "I hope you have a change of heart." I said, "In view of what's happening with Dr. Barney Clark in Salt Lake City (first artificial heart implant) did you have to say that?"

Friends from church, the Optimist Service Club, neighbors, and the school district who had had bypass operations called to encourage me.

The day before I entered the hospital, a solemn group gathered in my mother's comfortable living room. My brother Craig anointed my head with oil and brother Bob sealed the anointing and gave me a powerful blessing. They were assisted by Bishop James Wright and my home teacher, James Dunlap. Mother, kneeling by my chair, held one hand and I could feel the tears of Sondra on my other hand, held to her face. The heart and arteries were blessed to be made well quickly. Life was to have new meaning and direction. The healing was to be "remarkable," and I was to exercise faith. My family business and other interests were to be cared for. The blessing said not to worry, for I was loved by them and the Lord. So I entered the hospital four days after the angiogram, December 15, 1982, with faith and confidence that the Lord's will was being done and that all would go well.

The next morning Sondra, with a weak smile, squeezed my hand hard as I nervously entered the operating room. A dozen masked people kept me alive while they sawed my breastbone from neck to stomach, opened my chest, lifted and froze my heart, bypassed the blood flow with a machine, took veins from knee to ankle in both of my legs and cut them to size to make five bypasses in my heart. They sewed up my chest and took me to Intensive Care eight and a half hours later to regain consciousness.

As I struggled slowly to awaken, my mother and Sondra entered the ward and almost fainted. My color was pasty white, I was hooked up to several machines and bottles with tubes and wires infused into many parts of my body. When Sondra took my cold hand I squeezed as hard as possible. Only then did she know I would live.

After she went home that evening, a tired, worried Sondra wondered about me and what kind of a Christmas the family would have. As she drove into the driveway, she could see the glimmering lights of a beautiful decorated tree. She discovered that friends and visiting teachers had spent most of the day in our home making Christmas preparations.

The next day and those that followed was spent thanking the Lord and appealing for help. Jesus Christ was the focus of my prayers and thoughts. The theme of the most recent general conference had been on Christ and He had been the subject of my church talks since then. Yes, I was grateful for family, bishop, home teacher, and blessings, but Jesus Christ was the recipient of most of my gratitude for the restoration of the priesthood healing power and for His own suffering, atonement, crucifixion, and resurrection. I felt His blessing and His presence, as my healing began.

The hospital room was full of plants, flowers, cards and "too many visitors." My family visited in their Sunday best and within five minutes Joey knocked a plant on the floor, John Allen shouted to the nurses over the intercom, and Mark pushed bed "control" buttons which gradually squashed me. He also pulled out my monitoring wires. As the nurses rushed in, the family left. Feeling that recovery would truly be "remarkable" I thought, Wouldn't it be nice to have a miracle take place so that I could truly be healed quickly and I could end my book with a sensational, personal experience of healing? Oh, I wish that thought had never entered my mind!

When I went home for Christmas Eve a week later everything was functioning perfectly except for pain when I used my right leg. As I had been promised in the blessing given to me my heart and arteries did well, but the leg got worse and kept me from the physical activity I needed for a full recovery.

Lying in bed with my foot in the air day after day caused me, again, to turn to the Lord with fervent, humble prayer. The bishop and my son, Karl, gave me a blessing for the sore leg and confirmed the previous blessing of my brothers. I had hesitated to ask for another blessing believing that one blessing is sufficient for most health occurrences, but the bishop had volunteered to give me a blessing for what he believed to be a new problem.

From then on my leg got better, but ever so slowly. There was plenty of time to pray and search my soul as to the reasons for my plight. Why was I allowed to have diseased arteries? What was the purpose of having open-heart surgery? Was there a generic time capsule that indicated my time to die? Was I to learn humility; become closer to the Lord; learn more about diet and exercise to help myself and family in the future? Perhaps I would have more empathy for others, or gain insight into writing a book on blessings. Could I possibly be punished for seeking a miracle, or attempting to record sacred blessings? Could all that was happening simply be one of life's accidents or an injustice? Where had I failed to follow the Lord's will? What should be done now?

From all these thoughts—and many others through prayer— came an over-riding primary goal of wanting to live many more years and only do for myself and family that which I was foreordained to do. To me this meant to live the gospel to its fullest and to meditate and pray often over various alternatives of life's decisions.

There is purpose in illness. Satan can inflict accidents or disease to thwart us from inspired goals. Faith, works, and priesthood healing can cast Satan's physical and spiritual influence from us. Many are better people for having suffered. The apostle Paul wrote, "Though he were a son, yet learned he obedience by the things which he suffered." Those who cannot overcome the natural depression that comes from prolonged illness need extra help from loved ones, and they need blessings.

Because of the phlebitis in my leg, I began rehabilitation at Memorial Hospital a month late. I was back on blood pressure medication and very weak, but after two months of rehabilitation I was jogging three miles five days a week, and I had returned to my weight-lifting routine which was forty minutes three days a week. The weekly lectures at the hospital helped me to better understand diet, exercise, and handling stress.

Sometime later I viewed a live, open-heart surgery that was shown on public television one evening. The surgeon sliced through the patient's skin and took what looked like a Black and Decker ripsaw to cut through the breast bone. With my arms tightly folded across my chest as I watched the surgery I became squeamish by myself, so I got my son Michael to watch the remaining two hours with me. Since viewing "The Operation" I wonder now if I could have gone through with it without the Lord's direction.

The daily exercise along with the elimination of red meat and certain other fats from my nearly salt- and sugar-free diet brought me renewed health, lower blood pressure, and a good feeling about myself. I was ready to return to a modified better life. In fact, my goal was to run in my first race ever—a 5K sponsored by the Long Beach City College Institute. Then, as happens to many who are recovering from illness, I got knocked down again.

At the beginning of spring I began to experience a constant headache and nausea. I kept on jogging. That was now a part of my life, sick or not. Tests disclosed that I had hepatitis, probably contracted while I was in the hospital. The virus had had time to incubate and now my liver was painfully bloated from trying to rid my blood of serum hepatitus. The only helpful cure known is bed rest—and I had continued with my exercise program.

Thinking that my illness might be caused by medication, I stopped taking it. My blood pressure stayed low for a few weeks and, while I was still in bed, on my doctor's orders to overcome hepatitis, my blood pressure gradually rose to where medication was again prescribed.

My reaction was one of utter disbelief and then discouragement as the cycle seemed to repeat itself. Without a sense of progression I would answer close friends when they asked my condition with, "Terrible!" I missed, for the first time, the "Father and Sons" outing, I missed the 5K run, assigned meetings, playing with my children, and time at the store. All the questions, doubts—and now guilt for not doing my share—returned. It's difficult to imagine oneself as a patriarch in a home—let alone to act as one—when you feel rotten. It is imperative for parents to lead lives as healthy as possible or the children may suffer too.

The only thing for me to do was to—once again—pray, soul search, re-ask the questions, plead with the Lord, and fight the virus with rest and faith. I prayed, Lord, have I left out something? Did I not make the right decisions during the past months? I want to do thy will, but some things are out of my hands. Open the way, I'm prepared to enter. Just make me well. Should I seek yet another blessing for overcoming hepatitis? Is not this condition tied to the first blessing before surgery? My condition this time was more difficult for Sondra. She wondered if she could continue as Young Women's president, remain active on four P.T.A. boards, care for our children, and worry—again—about me.

It was more difficult this time for me to sustain a "mighty prayer." Many thoughts from my last illness had been justly discarded. The list of "doing thy will" was shorter. Life's alternatives were fewer. My mind was quieter. Had I missed something?

During the weeks that followed the hepatitis count lowered. I was still fatigued, but feeling better. The dizziness and stuffy ear similar to what I'd had five years before returned, probably caused by the rising blood pressure.

I was reminded that this humbling experience had caused me to make major changes in my life's goals.

In late spring, I drove to our family cabin in Lake Arrowhead to meditate and pray, "Lord, what wilt thou have me to do?" (Acts 9:6.) I also spent time concentrating on writing this book: to share with my family an understanding of why some are healed and some are not; to learn about the thought processes and actions involved in trying to do the Lord's will.

As I found myself writing more instructions to my children, rather than just stories for inclusion in the book, I recognized my intense desire to leave them my guidance in the event of an early death. My writings now had new meaning and I was excited about sharing my testimony of prayer and blessings with those I love.

On into the summer I wrote and edited a little every day. My health gradually improved. I began to feel the full effects of the blessings and could "run and not be weary." Never before had I sustained the conscious desire for so long to do only the Lord's will. Sondra also pleaded for daily guidance in making the right decisions: "Oh, Father, how can we best serve thee and our family?" No major changes were made in our lives at this time, but there was a stronger desire to be better parents.

Subtle, inspired changes, however, slowly emerged within me as a result of all the illness, prayers, and striving. "For after much tribulation come the blessings" (D&C 58:4).

In late fall, as I watched my smaller children "trick-or-treating," I leaned against a tree and unexpectedly shed tears. I had suddenly recognized recent changes in my feelings and in my life style. The desire to be with family, to love and be loved, to help others who are sick or lonely welled up in my heart. From then on my listening habits went from news to music. Rocking a child to sleep replaced some T.V. viewing. Thinking more about others than self was truly gratifying. Communication with my wife flowed. Loving emotions flooded my more frequent prayers. Hymns about the Savior brought tears. Renewing friendships had a priority. Retiring early and running at sunrise became enjoyable. Life had slowed with quality!

Even though there were still decisions to be made and problems to solve, the confidence had returned that "all would go well." With a little effort on my part, I could do God's will and be a good father.

Yes, fathers can work long hours, fulfill church assignments, have hobbies and be involved in the community as long as the needs of wife and children come first. Providing the necessities of life is fulfilling basic needs, but to enjoy quality time with the family is more important. President David O. McKay said, "The truest source of happiness will be found in the home." To preside at family gatherings, teach, pray and lead by example are musts for any father/patriarch. A priesthood bearer also has the privilege and responsibility to lay hands on the heads of his family and bless them as often as the blessings are needed.

President Harold B. Lee said, "Remember . . . the most important of the Lord's work you will ever do will be the work you do within the walls of your own home."